Robert Frost

Lectures on the Centennial of his Birth

Robert Frost

Lectures on the Centennial of his Birth

LIBRARY OF CONGRESS   WASHINGTON   1975

Library of Congress Cataloging in Publication Data
Main entry under title:

Robert Frost: lectures on the centennial of his birth.

Lectures delivered by Helen Bacon, Peter Davison,
Robert Pack, and Allen Tate at a symposium held Mar.
26, 1974 in the Library of Congress under the auspices
of the Gertrude Clarke Whittall Poetry and Literature
Fund.
  Supt. of Docs. no.: LC 1.14:T18
  1. Frost, Robert, 1874–1963—Addresses, essays,
lectures. I. United States. Library of Congress.
Gertrude Clarke Whittall Poetry and Literature Fund.
PS3511.R94Z917   811'.5'2   74–30100
ISBN 0–8444–0148–X

Acknowledgments
From *The Poetry of Robert Frost* edited by Edward Connery Lathem. Copyright
1916, 1923, 1928, 1930, 1934, 1939, 1947, (c) 1969 by Holt, Rinehart and Winston,
Inc. Copyright 1936, 1942, 1944, 1945, 1951, (c) 1956, 1958, 1960, 1962 by Robert
Frost. Copyright (c) 1964, 1967, 1970, 1973 by Lesley Frost Ballantine. Reprinted
by permission of Holt, Rinehart and Winston, Inc.

For sale by the Superintendent of Documents, U.S. Government Printing Office
Washington, D.C. 20402 - Price $1.55
Stock Number 3016–00022

The Gertrude Clarke Whittall
Poetry and Literature Fund

The Gertrude Clarke Whittall Poetry and Literature Fund was established in the Library of Congress in December 1950, through the generosity of Mrs. Gertrude Clarke Whittall, to create a center in this country for the development and encouragement of poetry, drama, and literature. Mrs. Whittall's earlier benefactions include the presentation to the Library of a number of important literary manuscripts, a gift of five magnificent Stradivari instruments, the endowment of an annual series of concerts of chamber music, and the formation of a collection of music manuscripts that has no parallel in the Western Hemisphere.

The Poetry and Literature Fund makes it possible for the Library to offer poetry readings, lectures, and dramatic performances. The lectures in the present volume were delivered on March 26, 1974, at a symposium observing the 100th anniversary of Robert Frost's birth.

Contents

Remarks of L. Quincy Mumford,
Librarian of Congress

It is with a deep personal pleasure that I welcome you to the Library of Congress. We are come together to do homage to the memory of our nation's greatest poet of the present century, Robert Frost, who was born just a century ago today. The conference of distinguished speakers and the dramatic performances of Frost's works are supported by the Gertrude Clarke Whittall Poetry and Literature Fund, which over the years has made possible the presentation in this auditorium of many lectures, poetry readings, and other stimulating cultural events.

It is a special pleasure for the Library of Congress to be the host to the observance of the Robert Frost Centenary, for Mr. Frost, as many of you know, was, in a sense, one of us. In 1958–59 he served as Consultant in Poetry to this Library, enlivening all of Washington with wit, his unique penchant for posting directions in the corridors of power, and his Olympian views on poetry, the arts, politics, and life itself. From 1959 to 1963 Mr. Frost served as Honorary Consultant in the Humanities.

The incumbent Consultant in Poetry, Daniel Hoffman, will introduce the speakers on our commemorative program.

The first of our speakers is a distinguished classical scholar who will approach the work of Robert Frost down a road not taken by the rest of us, with our small Latin and less Greek. Helen H. Bacon began her study of those languages and their literatures at Bryn Mawr College, and she taught there, and at the Women's College of the University of North Carolina at Greensboro, and at Smith before coming to Barnard College where, since 1962, she has been chairman of the department of Greek and Latin.

Miss Bacon is the daughter of the poet Leonard Bacon, who was a longtime friend of Robert Frost's. She is the author of Barbarians in Greek Tragedy *and has collaborated with the poet Anthony Hecht in a translation, published in 1973, of Aeschylus'* Seven Against Thebes. *As many of you know, this work has just been nominated for a National Book Award in translation.*

෫෨

"In- and Outdoor Schooling"
ROBERT FROST AND THE CLASSICS

by Helen H. Bacon

> It takes all sorts of in- and outdoor schooling
> To get adapted to my kind of fooling.

WHEN A CERTAIN MISS FLETCHER, professor of Classics at Wellesley, tried to get Robert Frost's daughter, Lesley, to be precise about Latin syntax she provoked the following from him (in part).

> . . . scourge blight and destitution. . . . She is a bad woman.
> To hell with her piddling accuracy in Latin. I should know it
> could come to nothing lovely and to nothing lovely it came.[1]

Frost's commitment to mind was only equaled by his distrust of scholarship. Baffled by a poem of Emerson's he refused to look for enlightenment in college, which "he had just left . . . to improve his mind." He preferred to wait 50 years for the insight that made it possible "to deal with all but two lines of it."[2] Believing that metaphor is the heart of thought as well as poetry, he insisted that one must discover for oneself the often subtle and obscure analogy.[3] "Success in taking figures of speech is as intoxicating as success in making figures of speech. . . . The heart sinks when robbed of the chance to see for itself what a poem is all about."[4] Elizabeth Sergeant, alluding to this passage, refuses to explicate "Directive."[5] What have I undertaken to do but short circuit the irreplaceable experience and violate these mysteries?

Like Plato's Alcibiades, I can only claim the privileges of the symposium, pleading the intoxication which comes from several months' immersion in the poetry and thought of Robert Frost. Like Alcibiades I will say what I would not dare to say if I were sober, and like Alcibiades I assume that those who have also

3

undergone the mysterious encounter will not misunderstand me. In his words, "If there be any profane or uncultivated persons present let them stop their ears."

A few discussions of Frost's lifelong involvement with classical writers and his use of them in his poetry already exist. My debt to them is very great.[6] To this mostly excellent literature I can hope to make only a modest addition. The task of recording, let alone interpreting, every allusion, direct and indirect, in letters, lectures, interviews, and poems is enormous. I have no illusion that I have, or ever will, achieve it.

That Frost's education at Lawrence High School, at Dartmouth, and at Harvard was principally in Latin and Greek history, literature, and philosophy, and that he taught Latin as a young man, needs no further documentation. That he read and thought about Greek and Latin authors all his life was clear from his conversation, as well as from his letters and his talks.

In every period of his life the allusions slip out so casually that they go almost unnoticed, but when you follow them up you always discover that they are loaded with awareness of their context and its application to the subject he is discussing.

In November 1962 at the end of his last talk to students he "spoke" "Take Something Like a Star" and then commented, "By star I mean the Arabian Nights or Catullus . . . something way off in the woods."[7] The lyrics of Catullus, which he probably first read at Harvard, were still, for him, among the things which are like a star, to which we turn when we need something "to stay our minds on and be staid."

> Say something to us we can learn
> By heart and when alone repeat.
> Say something! And it says, "I burn."

Could you describe Catullus better?

In a commencement address at Dartmouth in 1955 he said, "You've got to have something to say to the Sphinx."[8] It is the only "classical allusion" in the talk. I wonder how many of his hearers, or readers, had the "intoxication of success" that comes with "taking" that figure of speech in all its fullness. The theme of the talk is the theme of Sophocles' two Oedipus plays. Frost sums it up in sly and homely language when he suggests that you should develop your mind so that "you can listen to almost anything without losing your temper or your self-confidence."[9]

The talks and letters (like his conversation) are permeated with such charged and knowing references. They are a sign of the degree to which Frost's thinking and feeling were also permeated by Greek and Latin literature, and they are enchanting examples of that fooling, that Socratically ironic pose of being "just ordinary," [10] which only several kinds of indoor schooling can detect. To quote Alcibiades again (in my own free translation):

> At first someone listening to Socrates might find his ideas slightly comic. The words and phrases in which he cloaks them are like the hide of an impudent satyr. He likes to talk about pack-asses, and smiths, and shoemakers, and tanners, and he seems to be repeating the same ideas and the same language, so that an inexperienced and undiscerning person might laugh at his ideas. But if one can open up his ideas and see what is within he will find them first rational, then genuinely spiritual, containing many parables of human excellence, and having the widest application, indeed bearing on everything that a person with humane aspirations should explore.

I cannot resist adding a few intriguing examples from the letters— two early, one much later. In 1913 writing to Frank S. Flint about his book of poems, *In the Net of Stars*, he praises "the beautiful sad figure of the title, which recurring in the body of the book . . . gives to the whole significance. We are in the net of stars to our sorrow as inexorably as the Olympian pair were in another net to their shame." [11] It takes a moment to realize the appositeness, as from poet to poet, of this allusion to the tale in the *Odyssey* of the adulterous lovers, Ares and Aphrodite, trapped and exhibited to the mockery of the other Olympians, in a net made by the cuckolded husband, Hephaestus. In classical literature the lame smith, Hephaestus, is the image of the artist who at whatever cost in pain and grief, imposes form on chaos, curbs impulse, and snares truth in the net of art. The tale itself is sung by the original of all poets in Western literature, Demodocus, the blind bard of the Phaeacians. In case you think Frost would not have subjected the text of Homer to such "close reading," I refer you to his discussion of a simile in the *Odyssey*—the exhausted Odysseus washed up on the Phaeacian shore, asleep under the dead leaves in the thicket, compared to a fire banked for the night in a lonely farmhouse. "There you have something that gives you character, something of Odysseus himself. 'Seeds of fire.' " [12] The *Odyssey*, as others have noted, was one of his favorite texts. "The first in time and rank of all romances" was his comment, when he listed it among 10 books that should be in every public library. [13]

5

In another letter to Flint he makes a sly Latin pun on Flint's name, *cor silicis*, heart of flint, as a way of chiding him for not corresponding.[14] It is not a common Latin phrase. Among the Latin authors Frost read, I have found it only in Tibullus 1. 1, 64.

Then there is a letter of 1951 to Louis Henry Cohn containing what Frost calls a "spurious collector's item"—a mildly off-color limerick based on a rare, because coarse, word in a thoroughly off-color and little-known poem of Catullus (XXXII). Frost was nearly 80, but he must have been fooling around with the Latin text to have produced such a complex philological joke. I will come back to Catullus, who certainly haunted Frost all his life. The letter continues with a mock Platonic fantasy about transmigration of souls.[15]

This is a small fragment of the evidence in the talks and letters that Frost read and pondered classical literature intensely and subtly all his life. But what of the poems? We have his word that "they were all written by the same person, out of the same general region north of Boston, and out of the same books, a few Greek and Latin, practically no others in any other tongue than our own."[16] And the man who said "The way to read a poem in prose or verse is in the light of all the other poems ever written"[17] would, I hope, give his blessing to this attempt to look at his poems in the light of Greek and Latin poetry.

The task is delicate. I have found few direct imitations of individual poems. "For Once, Then, Something" is in one of Catullus' favorite meters, the hendecasyllable—a fact, as far as I can ascertain, discovered by Reuben Brower and admitted to by Frost.[18] Frost's free iambic tetrameters often turn into glyconics, a meter common in Greek lyric and used by both Catullus and Horace. The fact that "Pan With Us" begins with a glyconic—"Pan came out of the woods one day"—could not have escaped Frost's schooled and sensitive ear. And some of his swifter iambic poems sound very like Catullus' and Horace's swift, light use of iambic rhythms. Direct allusions and obvious analogies are also rare, though perhaps not quite as rare as critics have asserted. And yet the allusions and the analogies are there to be "taken." To see the analogy, to make the connection, to note the human or inhuman unity that underlies the apparently disjoined worlds of the ancient Mediterranean and the country north of Boston, challenges our schooling, both indoor and out. It is part of Frost's "fooling," not to draw it to our attention, but to leave it for the properly schooled to discover. Frequently, as I hope to show, when it comes to classical literature, he seems purposely misleading. He likes to drop a clue in the form of an allusion to a passage in the Bible or English literature, which, while not in itself false, is not the whole story. But it distracts us from looking further, and so we miss the classical analogy that lies beyond. The King James Bible and the English poets are far more appropriate than pagan antiquity to the homely Yankee surface he likes to maintain. One of the most deeply guarded and cherished secrets of the poetry is the affinities, which are never identities, with classical poetry which this Yankee surface masks.

For a first example—what homelier words can you find than "fooling" and "schooling?" Not even a literary allusion here to suggest that there is something beyond them. But the ancient poets, particularly Plato (Aristotle quite correctly calls the dialogs poetry), Catullus, Horace, and Vergil, like to refer to the practice of their art as "play," in Latin *ludere, ludus,* in Greek *paizein, paidiá.* The stance is always ironic, with an implication that there is hardly anything more serious than this kind of play. It is perhaps as near as we ever come to reality. In his introduction to Robinson's *King Jasper*, Frost says "Give us immedicable woes—woes that nothing can be done for—woes flat and final. And then to play. The play's the thing. Play's the thing. All virtue in 'as if.'" [19] The idea of serious play also comes out in a letter to R. P. Tristram Coffin. "Life sways perilously at the confluence of opposing forces. Poetry in general plays perilously in the same wild place. In particular it plays perilously between truth and make-believe. It might be extravagant poetry to call it true make-believe—or making believe what is so." [20] But do we need anything more than "The work is play for mortal stakes" of "Two Tramps in Mud Time?" Fooling.

Then schooling. That is another preoccupation of the ancient poets. It goes with fooling. Greek *scholé*, from which our word school is derived, is usually translated leisure. The Romans called it *otium*. It suggests frivolity, but there is no creative life without it. Again, serious play. School is where we have the leisure to lead the life of the mind. When Phaedrus asks Socrates if he has leisure, *scholé*, to hear about his discussion with Lysias, Socrates replies, quoting Pindar, "Don't you think I would consider hearing about your pastime 'even more important than business'?" The same insatiable Socratic appetite for talk at the expense of business can be seen in "A Time To Talk." The poet refuses to go on hoeing when hailed by a friend from the road. "No, not as there is a time to talk." He leaves his work and goes up to the stone wall "For a friendly visit." In "The Vantage Point" the poet passes the day "amid lolling juniper reclined," contemplatively poised between the natural world and the world of the town. In "To The Right Person" not only does the District Schoolhouse represent "higher" education because of its elevated mountain situation, but, precisely because its doors and windows are tight-shut, and it cannot be entered

> . . . penitents who took their seat
> Upon its doorsteps as at mercy's feet
> To make up for a lack of meditation.

Higher education implies freedom for reflection—schooling in its original Greek sense. Lawrance Thompson frequently speaks of Frost's laziness. Certainly some of it was his fierce way of keeping space for the mind and the spirit to grow in—for *his* kind of schooling.

Perhaps this seems farfetched and overrefined—I hope that when you have seen a few examples of equally delicate treatment of classical material where the documentation is somewhat firmer you will be more inclined to believe the lengths to which he will carry fooling.

Before I go any further with individual poems, however, there is a general point that should be clarified—namely, the commonly held view that goes back to the first reviews of *North of Boston*, that Frost is a pastoral poet.[21] In the strict, classical sense Frost is not a pastoral poet, though there may be some broadened sense of the term in modern criticism in which it applies to him. Frost himself spoke of Vergil's *Eclogues* in connection with *North of Boston*.[22] "Build Soil," which echoes the first Eclogue, is subtitled "A Political Pastoral." A good deal has been made of Frost's remark to Cox, "I first heard the voice from a printed page in a Virgilian eclogue and from Hamlet." If what he was noting in the *Eclogues* was also in Hamlet, it was not the spirit of the pastoral. He is referring not to the special relation of man and nature that characterizes ancient pastoral, but, as Cox goes on to point out, to "images to the ear,"[23] what he elsewhere called "the sound of sense."[24] It is for this, and for the mime form, the poetic dialog or monolog, that he drew on the *Eclogues* and Theocritus' *Idylls*. Though Horace too, both in the lyrics, and in the satires and epistles, provides many models for this type of poem. He speaks of returning to people in *North of Boston* (after running away from them in *A Boy's Will*) "to show that I had forgiven them

8

for being people." [25] The brutal realities of "being people" which we find in poems like "A Servant to Servants" involve a struggle with an indifferent nature which is worlds away from ancient pastoral. As Reuben Brower has pointed out, the pathetic fallacy, which is central to the *Eclogues* and the *Idylls*, is the antithesis of Frost's view of nature.[26] The shepherds of Vergil and Theocritus have griefs, but they hardly ever do any of the real work of the farm, which is the substance of so many of Frost's poems. Their real occupation is singing and lovemaking. Most of them are poets in rather transparent masquerade. They do not have to take on nature because, in the world of pastoral, nature grieves with man's griefs and rejoices with his joys, wild animals grow gentle at the sound of the shepherd's magic flute, and the Golden Age of complete harmony of man and nature, which is proclaimed in the fourth Eclogue, is, if not quite here, at least on the way. Even when, as in "Two Look at Two," Frost comes closest to a sense of some harmony between man and nature there is always his "as if . . ."

> As if the earth in one unlooked-for favor
> Had made them certain earth returned their love.

Is not Pan's discovery that his pipes

> . . . kept less of power to stir
> The fruited bough of the juniper
> And the fragile bluets clustered there
> Than the merest aimless breath of air.

a declaration that henceforth instead of the pathetic fallacy we are going to have "as if" ("Pan With Us")? Frost's "as if" is a fine illustration of his remark that he was a "dualist in his thinking and a monist in his wishing." [27] The harmony of man and nature is a profound but unrealized wish. The mind knows that nature looks on us "with neither love nor hate" ("Stars").

In the pastoral world love rules.

> Omnia vincit Amor: et nos cedamus Amori.
> "Love conquers all things: let us too yield to love."
> (*Eclogues* 10.61)

It is in Vergil's *Georgics* that we find the farmer struggling with the harsh facts of nature. *Labor* takes precedence over *amor*. Not *omnia vincit Amor*, but,

9

Labor omnia vicit
improbus, et duris urgens in rebus egestas.
(*Georgics* 1.145–6)

When the Golden Age ended, "Harsh work conquered all, and the cruel conditions of poverty that drive men on." It is in the *Georgics* that the work which the farmer patiently expends upon the soil becomes a metaphor for art, the art of the poet and the art of the statesman—the world of the spirit which cannot conquer nature but can transcend it. It is in the *Georgics* that the tools of the farmer's art are assimilated to the weapons of the soldier's art (the word *arma*, which means both tool and weapon, is played on over and over, cf., "The Objection To Being Stepped On" and "From Iron"), where the parts of the plough and the construction of the threshing floor are dwelt on with the same loving detail as the ax-helve and the grindstone, and with the same awareness of their implications about the mystery of the relation of art and nature and of the farmer's work as one of the sacraments of that mystery ("Mowing," "A Tuft of Flowers"). It is in the *Georgics* that we find the passion for the texture of soil, for fallow and sown, for weeds and wildflowers, for crops and timber and fruit trees, the naturalist's eye and ear for frog and mole and bird, and cow and horse and bee, for weathersigns and seasons.[28]

Frost is more a georgic than a pastoral poet. His own references to eclogues in connection with the poems is perhaps another characteristic bit of fooling. There are two lines in "Build Soil" which show that he knows the difference between Vergil's shepherds and the real thing. The speakers are named for the characters of the first Eclogue. Meliboeus, a real farmer going broke, says to Tityrus, who speaks with Frost's voice,

> The Muse takes care of you. You live by writing
> Your poems on a farm and call that farming.
> . . .
> But have some pity on us who have to work.

In spite of his frequent and eloquent defense of taking it easy, Frost's "people" are the ones "who have to work."[29]

The farmer who takes it easy, the kind of farming that involves no real work, also appear in "Something For Hope." Here Frost recommends that the farmer let the forest take over a pasture in which meadow sweet and steeple bush are about to crowd out the "edible grass." Then, he says, all you have to do is wait until you can cut down the forest for lumber, and you will have pasture again.

> A cycle we'll say of a hundred years.
> Thus foresight does it and laissez-faire.
> . . .
> Patience and looking away ahead,
> And leaving some things to take their course.
> Hope may not nourish a cow or a horse,
> But *spes alit agricolam* 'tis said.

Hope nourishes the farmer. The Latin quotation is from an elegy of Tibullus (2. 6, 21) in which the poet is describing the lover whose "hope" of long-delayed fulfillment keeps him from going off on military service. What kind of "farmer" is "nourished" by the hope of a crop a hundred years hence? Frost has converted Tibullus' expression of the lover's or the farmer's "hope against hope" into an affirmation of the sustenance of the spirit that the poetic imagination can provide. The poet is fooling with his favorite notion of schooling—*scholé, otium*. It is worth noting that he has fitted the first half of a dactylic hexameter into his iambic tetrameter without violating the Latin quantities and has changed Tibullus' plural, *agricolas*, to singular, *agricolam*, simply, I believe, to avoid another "s" in the line.

Frost's sense of the violence and indifference of nature, inside and outside people, which no skill or devotion of man can totally subdue, links him not only to the *Georgics*. In its Epicurean form it is a leit-motif of Lucretius, to whom Frost alludes more often and more directly than he does to Vergil. Far from making him a modern, as has been suggested,[30] it puts him in a tradition that goes back at least to Sophocles' *Oedipus Tyrannus*—the tradition that sees man as both part of nature, doomed, like all things, to suffer decay, and, at the same time, by virtue of mind, transcending nature. Who is the voyager in "Reluctance," who having set forth upon a journey into the wilderness and climbed "the hills of view," comes "by the highway home," where he finds the sleepers who do not seek knowledge? Whose "feet question whither"? Whose heart rejects in anguish the knowledge reason has brought, the knowledge which is both the end of innocence and the acceptance of mortality? Oedipus, after journeying to Delphi on Mt. Parnassus and receiving Apollo's oracle there, then took the highroad "home" to Thebes, on those ever-questioning feet, which for Sophocles are just as pervasive a symbol of the search for knowledge as

11

the eyes. In Thebes, in contrast to the "sleepers," he confronted the riddle of mortality head on, and endured the treason to the heart which is the message of reason—"To go with the drift of things."

Is this an intentional parallel or merely an archetypical pattern of which the poet is unaware? Both "The Mountain" and "Directive" deal more fully and explicitly with the theme of Apollo and Parnassus, and, in addition, link it up with the spring of the Muses and with Dionysus, who shared Apollo's cult at Delphi.

Dionysus, like Apollo, is a god of music and inspiration, but he is also, and importantly, a god of wildness and instinct. Wildness is one aspect of nature's indifference, one of the sources of the terror with which Frost confronts life in "The Most of It." But we should remember that though the last words of that poem are "that was all," its title is not "The *Whole* of It" but "The Most of It." In this poem he protests that he wants something more than an *echo* of his love, he wants "counter-love, original response." There is also a poem called "For Once, Then, Something," which, oddly, seems to be about Narcissus, the youth who rejected *Echo*. Like Narcissus, the speaker looking into the well gets back only an echo, "Me myself in the summer heaven, godlike." But he does once get an intimation of something else, beyond. There is *something* to the nature of things besides impersonal force and the echo of oneself. Wildness can turn into poetry. In fact, there is no poetry without wildness. In "The Figure a Poem Makes," Frost speaks of the mystery of "how a poem can have wildness and at the same time a subject that shall be fulfilled. . . . It begins in delight, it inclines to the impulse" and only as it acquires form, achieves its "momentary stay against confusion." [31] Nobody knew this better than the Greeks. Pan turns the impulse to rape into the music of the syrinx. The Muses are goddesses of wild mountain springs—Castalia, Helicon, Pieria. Dionysus dances with his barefoot Maenads in the snows of the wild peaks of Parnassus, but he also harnesses leopards or panthers to his chariot. He is not the god of impulse run wild, as he so often appears in modern literature, but the god of impulse transmuted into art and therefore has every right to his joint cult with Apollo at Delphi on Mt. Parnassus.

It is this complex of motifs, the mountain, the spring, wildness, and art (which a classicist cannot help thinking of as Parnassus, the Muses, Dionysus, and Apollo) that one finds played on and elaborated in "The Mountain" and "Directive."

In "The Mountain" the sense of the wilderness is first suggested by the way the nameless town where the speaker has spent the night is cut off from the mountain by the magical barrier of the river. Also the fact that the mountain blocks the view of the stars to the west suggests that by being cut off from wildness the town is also cut off from insight. Not only is the mountain wild, but also "There is no proper path" to the top. Like all abodes of the Muses it is a sacred place, accessible only to the initiate. The poet looking up toward the summit says

> There ought to be a view around the world
> From such a mountain . . .

In "Reluctance" the traveler had

> . . . climbed the hills of view
> And looked at the world . . .

On Parnassus we find insight, if it be only "a momentary stay against confusion." And of course on top of the mountain is the mysterious spring, "Cold in summer, warm in winter," and the informant, that slow countryman with his slow team of oxen, still knows something about the nature of that spring, though he has never tried to see it.

> I don't suppose the water's changed at all.
> You and I know enough to know it's warm
> Compared with cold, and cold compared with warm.
> But all the fun's in how you say a thing.

The spring of the Muses is an illustration of their particular brand of fun or fooling. The scattered farms on the mountain belong to the town of Lunenburg. The place has a name and a culture. But there is an ambiguousness about the name of the mountain. "We call it Hor: I don't know if that's right." To add to the mystery, I have it on the authority of the retired town clerk of Lunenburg, Vt., that there is no Mt. Hor near Lunenburg. In the poem, Lunenburg is a place apart,

> . . . no village—only scattered farms.
> We were but sixty voters last election.
> We can't in nature grow to many more:
> That thing takes all the room!
>
> . . .
>
> Hor is the township and the township's Hor.

13

The mountain overlooking the ancient city of Petra is named Hor. Moses' brother, Aaron, the priest and orator of the Israelites, is said to have died on its summit (*Numbers* 20: 22–29). It is a good Old Testament name for a New England mountain. A little farther north on Lake Willoughby there is both a Mt. Hor and a Mt. Pisgah—"hills of view." In the Lawrence *High School Bulletin* for December 1891 there is an essay by Robert Frost entitled "Petra and Its Surroundings," which begins, "On the summit of Mt. Hor, nestles a shrine beneath which, the Arabians say, lie the bones of the priest, Aaron. It is a place of the wildest grandeur—one worthy the last resting place of the Israelitish orator, overlooking as it does the mountain fastnesses of the warlike sons of Esau, through whose country the Jews strove so long in vain to force a passage." [32] A place of words, and a place of view, which Frost has transplanted to Lunenburg, Vt., and merged with the classical place of view, Parnassus. The last mystery about the mountain is that when the countryman with the oxen is asked if he has lived there all his life he answers,

> 'Ever since Hor
> Was no bigger than a ——' What, I did not hear.

Like the neighbor in "Mending Wall,"

> Bringing a stone grasped firmly by the top
> In each hand, like an old-stone savage armed.

he seems to go back in geologic time to the beginnings of things, to speak for a human spirit that transcends the nameless town across the river and is coeval with the mountain.

In "Directive" the theme of the spring of the Muses and its attendant imagery of Dionysus and Apollo is even more developed. I have been at least partly anticipated here by Elizabeth Sergeant, who when speaking of the poem refers to "an arcane spring, perhaps Pierian," and then, in a passage I have already quoted, refuses to explain further. [33] In a different way I have also been anticipated by Theodore Morrison, who explicates "the source" in the poem as "poetry in the largest sense," which is of course what the spring of the Muses represents in antiquity. The poem begins with going "Back in time," and continues by going back into geological time. As in "The Mountain," which also evokes a past as ancient as the mountain itself, the goal of the journey is a mysterious spring at the summit, to which there is no real path. The guide "only has at heart your getting lost." The mountain is called Panther Mountain. The panther or leopard, which Dionysus harnesses to his chariot is, as I have already pointed out, a symbol of the power of art to give order and direction to wildness and impulse. The mountain has gone back to wilderness. But just as Mt. Hor contains the remnants of a town, Panther Mountain was once the site of *two* "village cultures" which

> . . . faded
> Into each other. Both of them are lost.

I suggest that this refers to the twin cults of Apollo and Dionysus at Delphi, now lost in the past, like the "pagan mirth" of "Pan With Us." Lost, but recoverable "if you are lost enough to find yourself." If you are, then you are entitled to enter the world of the mystic fellowship of the Muses.

> . . . pull in your ladder road behind you
> And put a sign up CLOSED to all but me.
> Then make yourself at home.

Only after this comes the world of art, play, fooling.

> . . . the children's house of make-believe,
> Some shattered dishes underneath a pine,
> The playthings in the playhouse of the children.
> Weep for what little things could make them glad.
> Then for the house that is no more a house,
> . . .
> This was no playhouse but a house in earnest.

The "real" house is gone for good, but,

> Your destination and your destiny's
> A brook that was the water of the house,
> Cold as a spring as yet so near its source,
> Too lofty and original to rage.

The ultimate mystery—the Muses' spring, that something "more" that originates in wildness, but transcends mere wildness—the "momentary stay against confusion." Here is kept the sacramental cup,

> A broken drinking goblet like the Grail
> Under a spell so the wrong ones can't find it,
> So can't get saved, as Saint Mark says they mustn't.

"The wrong ones," who "can't get saved," are the profane, the uninitiated into the cult of the Muses, those who do not know about "true make-believe." The goblet is the goblet of "true make-believe" stolen from the children's playhouse. The last two lines are a true salute to Apollo, who as god of harmony is also god of medicine, of healing, both of body and of spirit.

> Here are your waters and your watering place.
> Drink and be whole again beyond confusion.

Apollo and Dionysus share the cult at the spring of the Muses on Panther Mountain, as they did on Mt. Parnassus.

Like the allusion to Mt. Hor in "The Mountain," the allusion to the Grail and St. Mark are not so much false clues as a way of preserving the New England tone while at the same time hinting at a mystery beyond. The journey up the mountain, beyond rage, to the source is certainly a journey into the poet's past, a deeply personal experience in which the Grail is a symbol of individual salvation.[34] But, in addition, it is a journey to the spring of the Muses on Mt. Parnassus, where salvation is achieved through reintegration not just with the poet's own past but with the ancient tradition of poetry.

As a footnote to this interpretation, I cannot help speculating about why both on Mt. Hor and on Panther Mountain, at the last stage of the journey even the vestiges of the path are gone. On Mt. Hor there are only "Great granite terraces . . . Shelves one could rest a knee on getting up." On Panther Mountain it is a "ladder road" that leads to the "height of the adventure." Is Frost evoking Apollo's devotee, the priestess Diotima in Plato's *Symposium* (a healer who kept the plague from Athens for 10 years), when she expounds love's "Greater Mysteries" to Socrates as an ascent "as though by steps" from the particular to the universal and transcendant beauty, which culminates in spiritual procreation? Frost frequently denied being a Platonist, but like Vergil (who was not a Platonist either) he often Platonizes for poetic purposes. "Trial By Existence," as others have noted, refers to the myth of Er in the 10th book of Plato's *Republic*.[35] I do not think it has been noted that it also echoes the Platonizing scene in Elysium in the sixth book of the Aeneid. "The Master Speed" paraphases the myth of the soul in *Phaedrus*. It would be hard to say whether "On a Bird singing in Its Sleep" is playing more with the theory of evolution or the Pythagorean-Platonic theory of transmigration of souls. In my opinion it is part of Frost's "fooling" to superimpose the one on the other. He also brings Darwin and Plato together in "Accidentally On Purpose," where he counters the mechanistic hypothesis of the *Origin of Species* with the deeply Platonic

> Grant me intention, purpose, and design—
> That's near enough for me to the Divine.

As a monist in wishing he sometimes found Plato irresistible. Think of

> There was never naught,
> There was always thought.
> ("A Never Naught Song")

The Platonic allusions in "The Mountain" and in "Directive," if they are really there, reinforce Morrison's point that "Directive" expresses Frost's view that the ultimate revelation of poetry and philosophy is the same. "Greatest of all attempts to say one thing in terms of another is the philosophical attempt to say matter in terms of spirit, or spirit in terms of matter, to make the final unity. . . . it is the height of poetry, the height of all thinking." [36]

After this it will perhaps not seem too improbable if I suggest that Frost, in another characteristic bit of fooling, implies that the Hyla Brook is to his New Hampshire farm what the *Fons Bandusiae* was to Horace's Sabine farm (Odes 3.13)—an ordinary water course in a humble alien setting far from Greece, transformed by its owner's powers of song into another spring of the Muses. Horace's 16-line ode celebrates a ritual, an offering of flowers, wine, and a young goat to the spring, probably on the day of the *Fontanalia*, the peasant Feast of Fountains, October 12. It preserves an almost homely rural Italian surface without literary references or direct allusion to the Muses. The young goat to be sacrificed has budding horns which proclaim him ready for love and battle, but "In vain: for the offspring of the lustful herd will stain with his red blood your icy streams." The wild Dionysiac impulse (the goat is also sacred to Dionysus) will be deflected and transformed in the waters of the spring. Lust and violence will become song. The spring itself, which never fails to offer refuge and refreshment, even in the hottest days of the Dog Star, is then saluted by the poet, "You too shall become one of the fabled fountains (i.e. Castalia, Pieria, Helicon) when I sing of the live oak that overhangs your hollow rocks, from which leap down your voluble waters." The waters themselves have a voice, they are *loquaces,* and the song of the poet has given his little Italian spring a place among the famous springs of the Muses in Greek literature.

"Hyla Brook" is one line shorter than *Fons Bandusiae.* Frost's brook also has, or had, movement and a voice. "By June our brook's run out of speed and song." But in deliberate contrast to the *Fons Bandusiae* it disappears in hot weather, taking with it all the singers, the Hylas or spring peepers. While the Italian spring continues to shine "brighter than glass," *splendidior vitro,* the vanished Hyla Brook seems to have "flourished and come up in jewelweed."

> Its bed is left a faded paper sheet
> Of dead leaves stuck together by the heat—
> A brook to none but who remember long.

The voice is gone for the moment, but the paper on which songs are inscribed is there. (If Frost can see "A Patch of Old Snow" as newsprint I think he can see the "faded paper" of the brook bed as the text of a poem.) The brook still brings refreshment to those who can remember. The Muses, *we* should remember, are the daughters of Memory, and the spring song of the Hylas also evoked memory "Like ghost of sleigh bells in a ghost of snow." The next two lines are another inversion. Horace's "You too shall become one of the fabled fountains," appears as

> This as it will be seen is other far
> Than with brooks taken otherwhere in song.

But different as it is, this brook too has been "taken in song" and has shown that it can nourish the spirit through the dog days. And then the last line—"We love the things we love for what they are." So Horace would rather sing of his little Italian spring than of Castalia.[37]

One other spring of the Muses is the pasture spring of the introductory poem of *North of Boston,* "The Pasture"—the poem which became, as it were, his signature. He used it as the introductory poem for all the collected and selected poems that appeared during his life, and, appropriately, it appears in the same place in Edward Connery Lathem's *The Poetry of Robert Frost.*[38] The "You come too," whether it be addressed to a friend or a lover, is an invitation to a comrade in the fellowship of the Muses to join him in contemplating a twofold mystery—the unquenchable spring and the miracle of creation in the form of the just-born calf. It is interesting that in what might be called his theme song, Frost's tone is again more georgic than pastoral. The participants are not poets in masquerade. It is a real farm scene, which symbolizes art.

The Horatian references in "Triple Bronze" (Odes 1.3), "Carpe Diem" (Odes 1.11), and "Auspex" (Odes 3.4) are more obvious than those of "Hyla Brook" but play the same game of inversion. "Triple Bronze" echoes Horace's address to Vergil, in which he suggests that the artist venturing into the uncharted worlds of the spirit, like the first men to go to sea, needs a heart encased in oak and triple bronze. Frost of course describes walling the infinite out, rather than setting out to explore it, but both poets are talking about the power of art and the spiritual force required to deal with chaos. "Carpe Diem" shifts the emphasis from the uncertainty of the future to the way in which the confusion of being young makes it almost impossible to seize the day. "Auspex" recounts an adventure in the Sierras when he was a little boy. Jove's bird of prey, the eagle, swooped down on him and almost carried him off like Ganymede. When the little Horace strayed from home and fell asleep in the wild mountains beyond his father's farm in Apulia, doves covered him with leaves to protect him from beasts of prey. Each poet takes his childhood encounter with the bird world as a portent of what he is to be—fostered by doves, repudiated by an eagle!

Frost's involvement with Horace, Catullus, and the Greek lyric tradition in which they worked is too complex and pervasive to demonstrate in detail. "Mowing" provides a comprehensive illustration. In a less obvious way than "Prayer to Spring," or "Rose Pogonias," or "Directive," or, in quite another mood, "A Record Stride," it describes, or reenacts, a ritual, as do so many of Horace's odes, including *Fons Bandusiae*. The fact that a mystery is being celebrated is indicated by the way the whispering of the scythe frames the poem and raises its central question. It whispers, "something about the heat of the sun," or

> . . . about the lack of sound—
> And that was why it whispered and did not speak.

Part of the mystery is the soundless action of the sun that ripens the hay. But there is more. The poet insists that the message of the ritual of mowing, whatever it is, is no dream.

19

Anything more than the truth would have seemed too weak
To the earnest love that laid the swale in rows,
Not without feeble-pointed spikes of flowers
(Pale orchises), and scared a bright green snake.
The fact is the sweetest dream that labor knows.
My long scythe whispered and left the hay to make.

The "fact," here so tenderly presented in terms of a New England hayfield, is the central fact of most of the Mediterranean agricultural mystery cults—there will be no harvest unless the flowers die. Adonis dies, Attis dies, Persephone picking flowers in the fields of Enna is carried off to Hades. The flowers must go before the hay can make. The snake, that equally widespread symbol of potency and rebirth, while startled, glides off, affirming the death of virginity and the promise of the harvest. With the single word "love," Frost has, as the myths I have mentioned do, linked the fertility of the fields to sexual and spiritual procreation. With so pervasive an image as this it is not possible to pinpoint the source. I can only say that my immediate association is to the broken flower, which represents virginity in the wedding songs of both Sappho (fr. 151)[39] and Catullus (LXII, 39–48), and to Catullus' poignant comparison of betrayed love to the flower at the edge of the meadow cut down by the plow (XI). The flower destined for sacrifice to the harvest also appears in "Rose Pogonias," "Spring Pools," "The Quest of the Purple-Fringed," and in a very special form in "The Tuft of Flowers," where the flowers which were spared by the scythe of the early morning mower carry the georgic message that the farmer's work symbolizes art, which transcends the order of nature and can establish "brotherly speech" not only between the absent but even between the living and the dead.

There are many aspects of Frost's indoor schooling in Greek and Latin literature that I have only touched on, others that I have completely omitted, such as the Lucretian vision of some of the poems about science, his adaptations of the techniques of Horace's satires and epistles in the long discursive poems ("New Hampshire," "Build Soil," "Lesson For Today," "How Hard It Is to Keep From Being King"), and the themes from Greek tragedy that underly the apparently biblical "A Masque of Reason" and "A Masque of Mercy." I would like to end with one more poem about the fellowship of art, which is also a particularly deft example of the kind of schooling and fooling I have been discussing—"The Lost Follower."

It is apparent not only from the title, but from the structure of the poem, that Frost is evoking Robert Browning's "Lost Leader."

> Just for a handful of silver he left us,
>   Just for a riband to stick in his coat—
> Found the one gift of which fortune bereft us,
>   Lost all the others she lets us devote.

Browning is talking about a poet, whom he always refused to identify, who abandoned the company of true poets for money and recognition. He goes on to contrast the power of gold, which enslaves, with the power of poetry, which liberates—evoking the spiritual fellowship of Shakespeare, Milton, Burns, and Shelley. He mourns for the leader, irrevocably lost in this life, but envisions a reunion and reconciliation with him after death.

> Then let him receive the new knowledge and wait us,
>   Pardoned in heaven, the first by the throne!

Frost's evocation of the poem is, characteristically, an inversion. Browning's mercenary leader has become an idealistic follower.

> The gold for which they leave the golden line
> Of lyric is a golden light divine
> Never the gold of darkness from a mine.

The young poet who deserts "the golden line of lyric" is trying, through politics or self-sacrifice, to achieve, what poetry has failed to do, bring about the Golden Age on earth. He does not understand that his ideal cannot be achieved as a physical reality, but may be found in the fellowship of the Muses,

> . . . right beside you booklike on a shelf,
> Or even better godlike in yourself.

Frost's poem, like Browning's, ends in heaven. Looking at his lost follower Frost sees

> . . . in the sadness in his eye
> Something about a kingdom in the sky
> (As yet unbrought to earth) he means to try.

But we are missing something if we stop with Browning, just as we are missing something if we stop with Mt. Hor in "The Mountain," or the Grail and St. Mark in "Directive." Horace's 16th Epode is about a world so full of greed, suffering, and violence that the only salvation is for the little band of the pure in heart (*pii*) to take ship and sail to the islands of the blessed. Again the poem ends in heaven. "Jupiter set this shore apart for the pure in heart, when he contaminated the Golden Age with bronze, . . . and then with iron made life harsh. From these misfortunes a happy escape is granted to the pure in heart, with me as their"—one expects pilot, but the word that comes is "bard" (*vate me*), a favorite word with Frost. Horace offers himself as the leader of an elect band who will discover in poetry the Golden Age which has vanished from the earth forever.

The "golden line of lyric," which Frost's young follower abandons in the hope of actualizing the Golden Age, is, I believe, a further and even more abstruse allusion to Horace's poem. The golden line is the name of a rhetorical device of the dactylic hexameter, described by Dryden in a classic passage as "that verse commonly which they call golden, or two substantives and two adjectives, with a verb betwixt them to keep the peace." (*Preface to Sylvae: Or the Second Part of Poetical Miscellanies*). The "golden line of lyric" might be thought to have nothing to do with this abstruse philological fact, since dactylic hexameter is usually classified as an epic rather than a lyric meter, though it is also the meter of pastoral, both Greek and Roman. However a good many of the Epodes use dactylic hexameters in combination with other meters, and of these the majority are lyrics. The 16th Epode alternates dactylic hexameters with iambic trimeters. The incidence of "golden lines" in the hexameters, particularly toward the end of the poem, is so much higher than "normal" that it is the subject of comment by scholars.[40] I have not been able to find out whether the conventional curriculum of Frost's student days would have included information about the golden line. But whether or not he learned about it as a student, it seems likely that he would have read Dryden's great essay on the art of translating classical poetry and noted his phrase about the golden line. I am as sure as one can be about anything for which there is no documentary proof that the "golden line of lyric" alludes to the golden lines of the 16th Epode. On that note of fooling and schooling I will make an end.

NOTES

I want to pay tribute of admiration and thanks to Kathleen Morrison, whose idea it was that a classicist should do a study of Robert Frost, and to Roy P. Basler, chief of the Manuscript Division, and Daniel Hoffman, Consultant in Poetry, both of the Library of Congress, for their parts in organizing and implementing the symposium for which this talk was prepared. I also want to record my warm thanks to Lawrence Rosenwald, a Columbia graduate student in American literature, for scholarly and bibliographical advice; to Harriet Lazer, a Barnard Greek major, for many kinds of assistance, both practical and scholarly; and to Leslie Sharpe, who produced a first draft typescript, working against time, and also generously provided invaluable professional editing and criticism. All citations of Robert Frost's poems are from *The Poetry of Robert Frost*, ed. Edward Connery Lathem (New York: Holt, Rinehart and Winston, 1969).

[1] Lawrance Thompson, *Robert Frost, The Years of Triumph, 1915–1938* (New York: Holt, Rinehart and Winston, 1970), p. 117.

[2] Robert Frost, *Robert Frost, Poetry and Prose*, ed. Edward Connery Lathem and Lawrance Thompson (New York: Holt, Rinehart and Winston, 1972), pp. 416–18.

[3] Frost, *Poetry and Prose*, pp. 329–40.

[4] Ibid., p. 417.

[5] Elizabeth Sergeant, *Robert Frost: The Trial by Existence* (New York: Holt, Rinehart and Winston, 1960), p. 394.

[6] In addition to the extensive documentation in the text, notes, and indexes of *The Early Years and Years of Triumph*, I have profited in some way from all of the following discussions, even though, in some cases, they are not directly referred to in my text. Lascelles Abercrombie, "A New Voice," Review of *North of Boston* in the English periodical, *The Nation* 15 (1914): 423–24. George O. Ackroyd, "The Classical in Robert Frost," *Poet Lore* 40 (1929): 610–14. Reuben Brower, *The Poetry of Robert Frost: Constellations of Intention* (New York: Oxford University Press, 1963). M. Camillucci, "Il Virgilio di Nuovinghilterra," *Persona* 4, no. 2 (February 1963): 18–19. John F. Lynen, *The Pastoral Art of Robert Frost* (New Haven: Yale University Press, 1960). Patrick Morrow, "The Greek Nexus in Robert Frost's 'West-Running Brook,'" *Personalist* 49 (1968): 24–33. Gorham Munson, *Robert Frost: A Study in Sensibility and Good Sense* (New York: George H. Doran and Co., 1927); "Robert Frost and the Humanistic Temper," *The Bookman* 71 (1930): 419–22; "The Classicism of Robert Frost," *Modern Age* 8 (Winter 1963–64): 291–305. Robert S. Newdick, "Robert Frost and the Classics," *Classical Journal* 35 (1940): 403–17. Edward H. Rosenberry, "Toward Notes for 'Stopping by Woods': Some Classical Analogs," *College English* 24 (1963): 526–28. Elizabeth Shepley Sergeant, "Robert Frost: A Good Greek out of New England," *Fire Under the Andes: A Group of*

Literary Portraits (Port Washington, N.Y.: Kennikat Press Inc., 1927), chapter 14.

[7] Frost, *Poetry and Prose*, p. 459.

[8] Ibid., p. 421.

[9] Ibid., p. 419.

[10] Ibid., p. 297.

[11] Lawrance Thompson, *Robert Frost, The Early Years, 1874–1915* (New York: Holt, Rinehart and Winston, 1966), p. 409.

[12] Frost, *Poetry and Prose*, p. 337.

[13] Ibid., p. 355.

[14] Thompson, *The Early Years*, p. 474.

[15] Robert Frost, *Selected Letters of Robert Frost*, ed. Lawrance Thompson (New York: Holt, Rinehart and Winston, 1964), p. 549.

[16] Frost, *Poetry and Prose*, p. 377.

[17] Ibid., p. 412.

[18] Brower, *The Poetry of Robert Frost*, p. 138. See note 6.

[19] Frost, *Poetry and Prose*, p. 353.

[20] Ibid., pp. 360–61.

[21] Particularly Lascelles Abercrombie and John F. Lynen. See note 6.

[22] Thompson, *The Early Years*, p. 428. Also Elizabeth Sergeant, "Robert Frost: A Good Greek out of New England," p. 299. See note 6.

[23] Sidney Cox, *A Swinger of Birches: A Portrait of Robert Frost* (New York: New York University Press, 1957), p. 109.

[24] Frost, *Poetry and Prose*, p. 261.

[25] Ibid., p. 378.

[26] Brower, *The Poetry of Robert Frost*, p. 80. Also Gorham Munson, "Robert Frost and the Humanistic Temper," p. 420, and "The Classicism of Robert Frost." See note 6.

[27] Thompson, *Years of Triumph*, p. 572, n. 25.

[28] Camillucci and Newdick (see note 6) comment on Frost's georgic tone but without analyzing it or distinguishing it from pastoral. If, in the body of his review of *North of Boston*, Ezra Pound had not referred to the poems as eclogues, I would have said he was very knowing when he entitled the review "Modern Georgics." *Poetry* 5 (1914): 127–30.

[29] G. R. Elliot, "The Neighborly Humor of Robert Frost," *The Cycle of Modern Poetry* (Princeton: Princeton University Press, 1929), chapter 8.

[30] Lynen, *The Pastoral Art of Robert Frost*, p. 162 ff. See note 6.

[31] Frost, *Poetry and Prose*, p. 394.

[32] Ibid., p. 201.

[33] Sergeant, *Robert Frost; The Trial by Existence*, p. 394. Also Theodore Morrison, "The Agitated Heart," *Atlantic Monthly* 220 (July–December 1967): 72–79.

[34] Mildred E. Hartsock, "Frost's Directive," *The Explicator* 16 (April 1958), Item 42. Also Brower, *The Poetry of Robert Frost*, pp. 233–42. See note 6.

[35] Thompson, *The Early Years*, p. 555, n. 4. In 1911 when Frost taught the history of education at Plymouth Normal School in New Hampshire, he threw away the textbook and substituted his own reading list. One of the books on that list was Plato's *Republic*. *The Early Years*, p. 372.

[36] Frost, *Poetry and Prose*, p. 336. For Morrison see note 33.

[37] Though Ackroyd (p. 613, see note 6) has very ingeniously found parallels with the myth of Hylas in this poem, I find myself unable to believe in them, since he cannot say what they express or even if they are intentional on the part of the poet.

[38] Frost, *Poetry*, p. 529, n. 1.

[39] So numbered in *Lyra Gracca*, vol. 1, ed. J. M. Edmonds. The Loeb Classical Library (Cambridge: Harvard University Press, 1928). Other editors use other numbering systems.

[40] See L. P. Wilkinson, *Horace and His Lyric Poetry* (Cambridge: Cambridge University Press, 1951), p. 146, n. 5.

Peter Davison, like Miss Bacon, comes from a literary family. His father, Edward Davison, was a poet too, and Peter Davison has ... written a personal memoir, Half Remembered, *in which he describes his education as a poet, which he owes to his father and to his friendship with Robert Frost during Frost's later years.*

Mr. Davison is familiar with Washington and its ways, having spent some time when a boy as a page in the U.S. Senate. After graduation from Harvard and study at St. John's College, Cambridge, he entered publishing and is now director of the Atlantic Monthly Press and poetry editor of the Atlantic. *His first book of poems,* The Breaking of Day, *won the Yale Series of Younger Poets Award in 1964. Selections from this and two subsequent books are to appear in his forthcoming volume,* Walking the Boundaries: Poems 1957–1974.

"Toward the Source"
THE SELF-REALIZATION OF ROBERT FROST,
1911–1912

by Peter Davison

THE CHARACTER OF ROBERT FROST, even more than other poets', flourished as a result of self-cultivation. The other huge figures of his era (Pound, Eliot, Stevens) or of the next poetic generation (Roethke, Berryman, Lowell) might lead us to think that all poets make themselves public in altered forms—shapes that resemble but only partly embody themselves. But we know better. A William Carlos Williams, an Elizabeth Bishop, do not feel the need to create cartoons of themselves like Eliot the Old Possum or Uncle Ez, the "village explainer."

Frost became the most popular, the most famous American poet since Emerson and Whitman, and like them the character he presented to the world was not the least, or even the least admirable, of his creations. It was constructed, as his very features were, out of materials that God had provided and was shaped as a result of events over which he had no control. But the Robert Frost whom I knew in his old age as a friend (closer than casual but not close enough for intimacy) contained in various proportions humanity and genius, jealousy and spitefulness, generosity, careerism, ease of access, and an ultimately obsessive secrecy. He was a man who on the one hand spoke to every acquaintance with the unaffectedness of a lifelong friend, but who on the other hand succeeded in concealing some of the important elements of his life even from his authorized biographer.

The fulfillment of Robert Frost's character led him very deep and took him a very long time. His maturing took something like 20 years to gather momentum and then washed him, very suddenly, up on the shore of himself. Most poets find their voices in their twenties. Frost had to wait, in irritable obscurity, until at the age of 37, through an act of conscious will, his character finally changed, deepened, and arrived. Three years later, on Washington's Birthday 1915, disembarking in New York after his sojourn in England, he found on a 42d Street newsstand, to his total surprise, a copy of *The New Republic* containing "The Death of the Hired Man." He was already famous.

In discussing Robert Frost's character I have chosen to concentrate on the few months before his English adventure, centering on January 1912, when I believe he lost himself and found himself at once. He never spoke much in his later life about this period, except in parables. As he wrote on his deathbed, "I'd rather be taken for brave than anything else," [1] and to the inner processes of self-transformation, bravery and cowardice do not exactly apply. The character he chose to embody in his middle and old age was one he had created as a form out of the deepest uncertainties. "When in doubt," he once wrote, "there is always form for us to go on with. Anyone who has achieved the least form to be sure of it, is lost to the larger excruciations." [2] He tried, without perhaps any better success than many of us, to make his life a poem. "Every poem," he wrote again, "is an epitome of the great predicament; a figure of the will braving alien entanglements." [3]

But to begin at the beginning. Robert Frost's first literary composition, when he was only a boy, was "a brief prose narrative based on one of his own dreams. Having run away from home, he climbed high among mountain peaks until he found a secret pass into a happy valley where he was welcomed [and honored as a hero] by some friendly Indians who invited him to stay." [4] He later renegotiated this theme into "The Bearer of Evil Tidings," [5] a poem whose poetic importance may loom less large than its psychological and biographical aspects. We don't put our childhood dreams behind us, we absorb them, we enact and reenact them, and if they mean enough and we have the power, we make them come true as Frost did. Even more significant, in my view, is Frost's poem "Directive," in which, as Theodore Morrison has suggested in his brilliant essay, "The Agitated Heart," [6] Frost gave us a parable for the road he took high among the mountains to find himself. "There," he said to one biographer, pointing to "Directive," "I rest my case." [7] The poem reads like a treasure map with a biblical legend:

Under a spell, so the wrong ones won't find it
And can't get saved, as Saint Mark says they mustn't.[8]

Robert Lee Frost was born in San Francisco on March 26, 1874. His father came from a very old New England family based in Lawrence, Mass. His mother had emigrated from Scotland at the age of 12. Both parents were teachers. William Prescott Frost, Jr., a cold, cruel, and humorless man, pressed marriage on Isabelle Moodie and took her west to San Francisco. Several years later they separated for a while, and Mrs. Frost took her two young children east to Lawrence for a stay of many months; but a reconciliation brought her back to San Francisco, where William Frost, city editor of the San Francisco *Post*, indulged in Copperhead politics, drank much whiskey, and visited various indignities on his wife and children. He died, in 1885, of tuberculosis. Again Mrs. Frost made the long journey east to bury her husband's body, by his request, in Lawrence.

From 1885 till 1911, except for two brief and unsuccessful ventures into college education at Dartmouth and Harvard, young Robert Frost lived mostly in, and never farther than 20 miles away from, Lawrence. When he was at home he slept in his mother's bedroom until at least the end of his high school years.[9] Witty, imaginative, proud, mystical, Isabelle Moodie Frost is probably the only person close to him of whom no one ever heard Robert speak an ill word.[10] In 1895, after a prolonged and intense contest of wills punctuated by suicidal threats and actions, Robert overcame his schoolmate Elinor White's doubts about his poor prospects. He forced her to consent to marriage before there was any assurance he would be able to support a family. He taught school at various places, still within the near magnetic radius of Lawrence, then went to Harvard for a little while but dropped out in 1899 when his mother became ill and a second child was expected. He returned to Lawrence again. During the year 1900 the pattern of his life was shattered. His eldest child Elliott died, partly as a result of the Frosts' medical naivete. A few months later his mother died as well. Meanwhile Frost's grandfather, William Prescott Frost, Sr., a stern but generous man (and incidentally an early convert to Women's Liberation), bought a farm for the young couple near Derry, N. H., 12 miles from Lawrence. In 1901 the grandfather died and left Robert an annuity in his will. These gifts of house and income young Frost was perverse enough to accept not as a franchise but as a sentence of banishment.

The Robert Frost who took up residence in Derry in 1900 was arrogant, touchy, neurasthenic, sickly, and shy. Contemporary photographs show us a smooth, stubborn, cold-eyed, sensitive face with sensuous lips, a face as different from the familiar face of our old poet as a blossom is from a wrinkled cider apple. His handwriting was indecisive, scattered, and slanting. He was preternaturally sensitive to slights and indignities and had long lived in resentment of his mother's long struggle against genteel poverty. In the poems he had already written, and in the poems he would soon write, he often speaks of running away, of losing himself in the woods. In fact this theme would repeat itself again and again from the first poem of *A Boy's Will* till the very last poem of *In the Clearing*. He was perhaps more troubled by the fear of weakness than by weakness itself. Lawrence and Methuen, Mass., Salem and Derry, N. H., these were all still foreign lands to the San Francisco boy. Years later in another poem he would have gained the wisdom to tell himself why:

> Something we were withholding made us weak
> Until we found out that it was ourselves
> We were withholding from our land of living,
> And forthwith found salvation in surrender.[11]

But the time was not yet. He had not yet found the courage to change, to surrender to "the unconsidered land," [12] the courage to be whole. He was not yet "on record as saying that freedom is nothing but departure—setting forth—leaving things behind, brave origination of the courage to be new." [13]

The years in Derry, N. H., 1900 to 1911, began in an atmosphere of terrible depression. The death of young Elliott had naturally depressed and embittered Elinor Frost as deeply as Robert. Frost's own versions of these years vary. As he said in old age, "Don't trust me too far. I'm liable to tell you anything. Trust me on the poetry, but don't trust me on my life. You want to watch me. Check up on me some." [14] I have chosen three from his many and varied descriptions of the Derry years, the first from 1913, written to his fellow poet F. S. Flint even before publication of *A Boy's Will*: "When the life of the streets perplexed me a long time ago I attempted to find an answer to it for myself by going literally into the wilderness, where I was so lost to friends and everyone that not five people crossed my threshold in as many years." [15] The second account dates from 1932:

For six months after we went to the farm I did nothing. The rugs were there, but I didn't put them down. The well was only twenty or thirty steps from the door. It would have been a simple thing to have piped it into the house, but during the entire eight years there we carried water. There was always a bucket in the sink.

I was ambition-less, purposeless. For months on end I would do no work at all. I didn't write because I wanted to write. I wrote because I wrote. . . .

During the entire eight years there no friend ever sat down within our home. . . . Friends never came. There were no friends. I sometimes think of those years as almost a fadeout . . . as an escape into a dream existence,[16] as in dementia praecox.[17]

The third account dates from 1935 and a public speech: "I remember ten or twenty years of writing after I wrote the first poem that I got any personal satisfaction from. [He means "My Butterfly: An Elegy," 1894.] Twenty years of it when I was out and in and didn't know what I was and didn't know what I wanted, nor what the feeling was that I wanted to satisfy. Not having anything in the mind, no formula, just seeking, questing."[18]

We know from Lawrance Thompson's massive biography that these versions of the Derry years are far from the whole story. By 1906 the worst of his depression was over, and Frost little by little emerged from his isolation, began teaching school again, became inventive as a teacher and revered by many of his students. He was writing, and sometimes publishing, poems. He began taking his family on summer holiday trips into the mountains of New Hampshire and Vermont. In 1909 the Frosts left the Derry farm to share a house in Derry Village. By now there were four children in a closely knit family. As Frost himself would write in 1912 when annotating the poems in *A Boy's Will*, "The youth is persuaded that he will be rather more than less himself for having forsworn the world . . . yet he resolves to become intelligible, at least to himself, since there is no help else."[19]

In 1911 as soon as the Derry farmhouse became available, under the terms of gift, for the Frosts to sell, they promptly sold it. During that same year Robert was invited to teach psychology at the Normal School in Plymouth, N. H., 65 miles to the north of Derry, deeper into the woods and mountains. Both the family and the poet found new friends at Plymouth. Among the most notable was Sidney Cox, a younger fellow teacher whom Frost could talk to as an equal yet depend on for deference and admiration. Robert seemed to be displaying a new confidence in himself, for reasons not immediately clear, reasons he himself never made explicit in later years. Lawrance Thompson reports:

> He now had the gait and carriage of a man going somewhere. . . . This very touchy man of moods . . . had brought his arrogance and grouchiness under at least temporary control. At Plymouth, in his offhand conversations inside and outside the classroom, his remarks were usually cheerful, witty, mischievous, playful. [Old friends] would have noticed that even his speech was different from his talk at the time of the move from Lawrence to Derry in 1900. . . . Frost had gradually modified his way of talking. He deliberately imitated the manner in which his neighbors unconsciously slurred words, dropped endings, and clipped their sentences. By the time he reached Plymouth, glad to be rid of the farm, he was still perfecting the art of talking like a farmer.[20]

So much for the outward signs of change or preparation for change. For the inward record we will have to turn to the poetry, for the biographers, and Frost himself, tell us all but nothing. "Directive," as you will remember, directs us "Back out of all this now too much for us," along a half-abandoned road to

> . . . a house that is no more a house
> Upon a farm that is no more a farm
> And in a town that is no more a town.

Not only is the poem "one of the most moving poems Frost or anyone has written," as Theodore Morrison rightly says, but its very esoteric quality offers a "riddling invitation to those who are capable of it to go, starting from confusion, back to whatever source their hearts venerate, and to find there the wholeness they may not have known since the forward journey innocently began."[21] Frost cannot speak to or for us unless he is also in some way speaking for himself, in "a figure of the will braving alien entanglements." "Directive" tells us much about rage and division, about moving back from the present into the past, from the valleys to the mountains, into the psychically deserted New England culture. Can Robert Frost be suggesting, in the lines that conclude the poem, that he had found "wholeness" by returning to his own New England sources after a long resistance? That, "possessing what he still was unpossessed by," he had finally "found salvation in surrender?"

Your destination and your destiny's
A brook that was the water of the house,
Cold as a spring as yet so near its source,
Too lofty and original to rage.
(We know the valley streams that when aroused
Will leave their tatters hung on barb and thorn.)
I have kept hidden in the instep arch
Of an old cedar at the waterside
A broken drinking goblet like the Grail
Under a spell so the wrong ones can't find it,
So can't get saved, as Saint Mark says they mustn't.
(I stole the goblet from the children's playhouse.)
Here are your waters and your watering place.
Drink and be whole again beyond confusion.[22]

The external signs were all there in 1911: Frost's breakaway from Derry, his newly mannered speech, his evident confidence, his new cheerfulness and wit—all these must be taken as signs of self-definition, most particularly his new-found humor. "The style is the man," Robert Frost once wrote, "Rather say the style is the way the man takes himself; and to be at all charming or even bearable, the way is almost rigidly prescribed. If it is with outer seriousness, it must be with inner humor. If it is with outer humor, it must be with inner seriousness. Neither one alone without the other under it will do." [23] Frost's new style, like his new personality, was calculated to be both charming and bearable.

I think most critics would agree that, taken as a question of style alone, the principal differences between *A Boy's Will* and *North of Boston* reside in two particulars: first, the pronounced difference in tone, in the balance between inner and outer humor and seriousness; second, the quite revolutionary return, Wordsworthian and Emersonian in its boldness, to the sounds and rhythms of ordinary speech. Once the new style had been achieved and Frost knew he had mastered it, he minced no words, writing to John Bartlett on July 4, 1913: "To be perfectly frank with you I am one of the most notable craftsmen of my time. . . . I alone of English writers have consciously set myself to make music out of what I may call the sound of sense." [24]

I believe that before the end of the year 1911, in Plymouth, Robert Frost had begun "taking himself" differently enough to make this new style, this craftsman's revolution, possible. How conscious was the alteration? Just before Christmas 1911 he wrote to Susan Hayes

33

Ward, a woman old enough to be his mother. She had been encouraging him ever since 1894 when she published "My Butterfly: An Elegy" in *The Independent*. Frost's Christmas letter was filial both in its devotion and in its assumptions that Miss Ward cared as deeply about his fate as he did himself. He enclosed a manuscript booklet of 17 poems, nine of which would appear in *A Boy's Will* and later books.

> It represents, needless to tell *you*, not the long deferred forward movement you are living in wait for, but only the grim stand it was necessary for me to make until I should gather myself together. The forward movement is to begin next year. . . .[25]

A week or two later, over the Christmas holidays, Frost traveled to Newark, N. J., to visit Miss Ward. Immediately on his return, in January 1912, he began writing in a frenzy. Apparently he had meant it literally when he said "next year." His revolution was under way.

Before looking more deeply into the special quality of Frost's inner revolution, let us hear from a writer, Karl Marx, who, though alien to Frost, knew something of the nature of revolution in general:

> Men make their own history, but they do not make it just as they please; they do not make it under circumstances directly encountered, given and transmitted from the past. The tradition of all the dead generations weighs like a nightmare on the brain of the living. And just when they seem engaged in revolutionizing themselves and things, in creating something that has never yet existed, precisely in such periods of revolutionary crisis they anxiously conjure up the spirits of the past to their service and borrow from them names, battle cries and costumes in order to present the new scene of world history in this time-honoured disguise and this borrowed language. In like manner a beginner who has learnt a new language always translates it back into his mother tongue, but he has assimilated the spirit of the new language and can freely express himself in it only when he finds his way in it without recalling the old and forgets his native tongue in the use of the new.[26]

When Robert Frost returned from Newark at the New Year, 1912, he was deep into Henri Bergson's newly published *Creative Evolution*, which he had been reading on the train. In Bergson he found ready evidence to confirm the turbulent changes that were taking place in his own psyche:

> We trail behind us, unawares, the whole of our past; but our memory pours into the present only the odd recollection or two that in some way complete our present situation.[27]

Let us seek, in the depths of our experience, the point where we feel ourselves most intimately within our own life. It is into pure duration that we then plunge back, a duration in which the past, always moving on, is swelling unceasingly with a present that is absolutely new. But, at the same time, we feel the spring of our will strained to its utmost limit. We must, by a strong recoil of our personality on itself, gather up our past which is slipping away, in order to thrust it, compact and undivided, into a present which it will create by entering. Rare indeed are the moments when we are self-possessed to this extent: it is then that our actions are truly free.[28]

I doubt that Frost ever read the passage from Marx, but we know he read Bergson, probably with a throb of excitement at the prospect of being "truly free." Let these passages guide us in assessing Frost's interior struggle of January 1912, a month in which the poetry fit was on him.[29] In thanking Miss Ward after his visit to Newark, he hinted darkly, "Please remember who it was that Luther thought the proper target to throw ink at by the bottleful," [30] and he enclosed an early draft of "Design," his most diabolic sonnet. What was he writing during this aggressive expenditure of ink? One thing can be fairly proved: the poems written at this moment were not those later published in *A Boy's Will* but some that would go to make up the more revolutionary *North of Boston*, and some that would furnish Frost's later books.

The next letter Frost wrote Miss Ward was dated February 10. By this time a great deal of ink had been thrown at the devil. The letter does not mention any colors except light and darkness, and it is entirely lacking in sound images. Yet it contains in its phrases echoes not only of Bergson and Shelley but of half a dozen poems Frost had written, would write, and perhaps was writing at that very season.

Two lonely cross-roads that themselves cross each other I have walked several times this winter without meeting or over-taking so much as a single person on foot or on runners. The practically unbroken condition of both for several days after a snow or a blow proves that neither is much travelled. Judge then how surprised I was the other evening as I came down one to see a man, who to my own unfamiliar eyes and in the dusk looked for all the world like myself, coming down the other, his approach to the point where our paths must intersect being so timed that unless one of us pulled up we must inevitably collide. I felt as if I was going to meet my own image in a slanting mirror. Or say I felt as we slowly converged on the same point with the same noiseless yet laborious strides as if we were two

35

images about to float together with the uncrossing of someone's eyes. I verily expected to take up or absorb this other self and feel the stronger by the addition for the three-mile journey home. But I didn't go forward to the touch. I stood still in wonderment and let him pass by; and that, too, with the fatal omission of not trying to find out by a comparison of lives and immediate and remote interests what could have brought us by crossing paths to the same point in the wilderness at the same moment of nightfall. Some purpose I doubt not, if we could but have made it out. I like a coincidence almost as well as an incongruity.[31]

I am no professional interpreter of dreams, but I would find this letter quite amazing no matter who had written it. Coming from Frost it is stunning. Just as he had mythologized his years in Derry to make them sound more forsaken than the reality, so in this dream letter Frost has managed to construct a personal myth out of a chance meeting. But it looms even larger than that. As he "stood still in wonderment and let him pass by," Frost was some-how defining his life. Was he not rejecting one part of himself, making himself simpler but more controllable and more secretive, accepting the disguise which he had worked up in Derry and tired on in Plymouth, the disguise of countryman-philosopher-poet? He took on this disguise as an act of conscious will. But before long he grew into it, as the nymph Daphne turned into a laurel tree when pursued by the god.

Such a letter will have special meaning for the depth psychologists, but there is much in it that a mere student of poetry can respond to.

> What brought the kindred spider to that height?
> Then steered the white moth thither in the night? [32]

Who is the man whom Frost imagines to be himself, just as

> the Magus Zoroaster, my dead child,
> Met his own image walking in the garden? [33]

Could he be a dream image of the father whom Robert had last seen alive in San Francisco? Is it the past which he is willing to face, to "expect to take up or absorb . . . and feel the stronger?" Is it an alternative self which he is tempted to become? Do the two contrasting figures, "my own image in a slanting mirror," embody the angle of conflict between Frost's humanity and his poetry? Rather than hack the symbolism of the dream into a heap of shattered chips, let us simply note again that "I stood still in wonderment and let him pass by." It was the Grand Refusal.

Like many American writers Frost had been drawn from the West to the East. Henry James and Mark Twain, to name but two, had relished the eastward movement; Frost, up until this time in his life, had begrudged that motion eastward because to him it meant disgrace and failure. But now he had recognized the validity of Bergson's retrograde movement, "obliged, though it goes forward, to look behind," [34] and was willing to pay what he would later call "the tribute of the current to the source." [35] Now he inwardly accepted the retrograde movement, the existence of his past, and he found himself the stronger for it, whole at last. Wholeness so freed him, in fact, that he was able not only to liberate himself from Derry, that haunted place, but, a year later, to launch out on another great leap.

In the summer of 1912, when Robert's annuity under the terms of his grandfather's will increased from $800 to $1,000, the Frosts are said to have flipped a coin to decide whether to move to Vancouver or England. "The coin chose England," Frost reported.[36] What a coin! It pointed them toward the east, recapitulating the movement of 1885 from California; but this move eastward brought with it a tremendous access of new energy. Not a month after arriving in England and settling in Beaconsfield on the edge of London, Frost was at last able to dust off the poems in *A Boy's Will*—almost all of them except "one or two things to round out the idea" [37] long since completed during the Derry years—and take them to a publisher.

Throughout the fall of 1912 he went on writing poems, poems in his adopted Yankee voice, in the *North of Boston* style, giving himself over to his sense of New Hampshire language and landscape, to the gaunt people who lived in a sparse country where grass covered up the cellar-holes and snow covered up the grass. "You have no idea," he wrote to Sidney Cox at Christmas 1912, "of the way I mismanage myself since I broke loose and ceased to keep hours. It seems as if I did nothing but write and write. . . ." [38] By the late summer of 1913, a year after leaving the United States, not only was *A Boy's Will* already published, but *North of Boston* seems also to have been complete, and it was published in England the next year. Frost, between writing his letters to John Bartlett expatiating on "the sound of sense" and reveling in his newfound friendships with Edward Thomas and other English poets, marveled a little at what had happened to him. The change was evident in a dozen ways. His very handwriting altered significantly during the year 1912, showing new traits which a graphologist might identify as increases in both boldness and secretiveness. Frost had arrived not only at a new poetic style but at a new personality which the style reflected. The style was indeed "the way the man took himself," with "outer humor but with inner seriousness."

A few years later he would answer an inquirer's questions with more questions. "I wonder if coming to New England from California can have had anything to do with my feeling for New England and I wonder if my having written so much about it from as far away as old England can have helped?" And he dropped another hint about the relation between the change in personality and the change in style: "Look for something unsocial in A Boy's Will as compared with North of Boston." [39] Finally, when he wrote "The Bearer of Evil Tidings" he would relate the fulfillment of his childhood dream:

> At least he had this in common
> With the race he chose to adopt:
> They each of them had their reasons
> For stopping where they had stopped. [40]

For the moment he had stopped in England. At the age of 39 he knew himself to be among the notable poets of his time two years before the world would get around to finding out. Exulting in his craft, he was not yet given over to the entanglements of conspiracy and careerism. His family was still united and not yet blighted with catastrophe. The new wounds that success would inflict upon his marriage had not yet been struck. Though he had for decades been living the life of a poet, now at last he knew himself for one without having to teach, or to "bard around," or to connive at his reputation and advancement as he would later on. He could ramble the Gloucestershire fields with Edward Thomas and give himself as generously to friendship as he ever would again. He was withholding nothing. He had drunk at the spring. He was whole again without confusion. After that crucial winter at Plymouth, with its mysterious encounter at the crossroads, he had finally caught up with himself, after years of "hurling experience ahead of [himself] to pave the future with against the day when [he might] want to strike a line of purpose across it for somewhere." [41]

NOTES

[1] Robert Frost, *Selected Letters of Robert Frost*, ed. Lawrance Thompson (New York: Holt, Rinehart and Winston, 1964), p. 595.

[2] Robert Frost, *Selected Prose of Robert Frost*, ed. Hyde Cox and Edward Connery Lathem (New York: Collier Books, 1968), p. 106.

[3] Ibid., p. 25.

[4] Lawrance Thompson, *Robert Frost, The Early Years, 1874–1915* (New York: Holt, Rinehart and Winston, 1966), pp. xvii, 38.

[5] Robert Frost, *The Poetry of Robert Frost*, ed. Edward Connery Lathem (New York: Holt, Rinehart and Winston, 1969), pp. 313–14.

[6] Theodore Morrison, "The Agitated Heart," *The Atlantic* 220, no. 1 (July 1967): 72–79.

[7] Elizabeth Shepley Sergeant, *Robert Frost: The Trial by Existence* (New York: Holt, Rinehart and Winston, 1960), p. 395.

[8] Frost, *Poetry*, pp. 377–79.

[9] Thompson, p. 205.

[10] Morrison, p. 74.

[11] Frost, *Poetry*, p. 348.

[12] Letter to Louis Untermeyer in *Selected Letters of Robert Frost*, p. 387.

[13] Frost, *Selected Prose*, p. 115.

[14] Thompson, p. xiv.

[15] Elaine Barry, *Robert Frost on Writing* (New Brunswick, N.J.: Rutgers University Press, 1973), p. 86.

[16] Margaret Bartlett Anderson, *Robert Frost and John Bartlett* (New York: Holt, Rinehart and Winston, 1963), pp. 4–5.

[17] Thompson, p. 561.

[18] Sidney Cox, *A Swinger of Birches* (New York: New York University Press, 1957), p. 85.

[19] Frost, *Poetry*, pp. 529–30.

[20] Thompson, pp. 370–71.

[21] Morrison, p. 79.

[22] Frost, *Poetry*, pp. 378–79.

[23] Frost, *Selected Prose*, p. 65.

[24] Anderson, p. 52.

[25] Frost, *Selected Letters*, p. 43.

[26] Karl Marx, *The Eighteenth Brumaire of Louis Napoleon* (New York: International Publishers, 1963), p. 15.

[27] Henri Bergson, *Creative Evolution*, trans. Arthur Mitchell (New York: Modern Library, 1944), p. 184.

[28] Ibid., pp. 218–19.

[29] Frost, *Selected Letters*, p. 60.

[30] Ibid., pp. 44–45.

[31] Ibid., p. 45.

[32] Frost, *Poetry*, p. 302.

[33] Percy Bysshe Shelley, "Prometheus Unbound," i, 192.

[34] Bergson, p. 259.

[35] Frost, *Poetry*, p. 260.

[36] Thompson, p. 390.

[37] Frost, *Selected Letters*, p. 60.

[38] Ibid.

[39] Barry, p. 74.

[40] Frost, *Poetry*, p. 314.

[41] Frost, *Selected Prose*, p. 19.

Our third speaker is Robert Pack, who is Abernthy Professor of American Literature at Middlebury College, where he has taught for the past 10 years. He has published a critical study of Wallace Stevens and six volumes of verse, the most recent of which is Nothing but Light. *Mr. Pack is also director of the Bread Loaf Writers' Conference, which, as you know, was founded by Robert Frost. Accordingly, we look forward to what he will tell us of Robert Frost as teacher and preacher.*

~ॐ

Robert Frost's "Enigmatical Reserve"
THE POET AS TEACHER AND PREACHER

by Robert Pack

> ". . . I proposed to give one [course] in philosophy on judgments in History, Literature, and Religion—how they are made and how they stand, and I was taken on by the department [at Amherst] like odds of a thousand to one. Well the debacle has begun. Here begins what probably won't end till you see me in the pulpit." [1]

IN DESCRIBING one of his own poems, Robert Frost says that it has the "proper enigmatical reserve." [2] Frost believed that the surface of a poem, like speech, should be simple and immediate, yet upon further scrutiny, the poem should reveal itself as elusive. After all, life does not readily yield up its meaning and purpose—indeed, if it has any. The poet must be as accurate as he can in describing his sense of the mysteries of nature and of God, and he must be true to his own "confusion"—to use one of Frost's favorite words. What the poem contains is not merely private knowledge but the poet's own uncertainty, and the order the poem imposes on this uncertainty functions to dramatize, not simplify or dismiss, what it is that puzzles Frost. As he says, "I don't like obscurity or obfuscation, but I do like dark sayings I must leave the clearing of to time." [3] If Frost as poet is also to be thought of as teacher and preacher, then we, as readers, must regard his poems as if they are parables. His poems speak most profoundly when they speak by indirection. They are indeed "dark sayings," engagingly "enigmatical." And the best of them maintain Frost's characteristic "reserve."

The dark qualities of a Frost poem, however, do not necessarily determine that the poem will be without humor. There is often

43

an element of playfulness even in Frost's most serious poems. The play of the poem, the poet's power to create a design, are what Frost summons to contend with darkness and confusion. He takes delight in the resistance to uncertainty and disorder that humor can provide. About "The Road Not Taken,"[4] Frost says, "it's a tricky poem, very tricky."[5] Frost has his own games to play with the game life demands that he play:

> Forgive, O Lord, my little jokes on Thee
> And I'll forgive Thy great big one on me.[6]

Frost's poems, then, are "tricky" out of a mischievious sense of delight in the intricacies of tone and image that a poem can organize, and "tricky" in that they themselves resemble the dangerous paths toward possible forgiveness and salvation which man must choose to follow in the course of his days. The image of the road appears in many poems, but it is always uncertain as to what revelation the road leads to, even when the destination or place is as specific as the "frozen wood" in "The Wood Pile"[7] or the old couple's new home in "In the Home Stretch."[8]

Frost begins his poem "The Oven Bird"[9] with a playful and strategic lie. "There is a singer everyone has heard," he says. A reader, unaccustomed to Frostian trickery, will simply accept this line for what it states, but Frost knows perfectly well that not every reader has heard the call of an oven bird. And certainly no one has heard an oven bird that says "leaves are old" or "the early petal-fall is past" as he does in this poem. Frost is playing a game here with the reader's credulity, for the question of what we can believe on the basis of the little that we can know is precisely the problem Frost is exploring here. What Frost is leading the reader toward, Reuben Brower calls "felt truth . . . a revelation of which the meaning is the unfolding poetic event."[10] Although the literal sound the bird makes is described merely as "loud" and is, in this sense, distracting, Frost invites the reader with him to "make" of this sound some speech that is humanly useful. Nature only speaks when man makes it speak. What man believes, beyond what he hears and sees, is necessarily of his own invention.

The oven bird's milieu is "mid-summer" and "mid-wood," yet the bird speaks of the "highway dust." Both man and bird, as it were, are midway in the journey of their lives, and though this road inevitably leads to dust and death, what matters most is the kind of song that man freely chooses to sing along the way. As

Emerson says, "In popular experience everything good is on the highway." [11] (And Frost comments about Emerson, "I owe more to Emerson than anyone else for troubled thoughts about freedom.") [12] The poet, lying his way hopefully toward the truth, tells us the bird "makes the solid tree trunks sound again." But this new sound becomes the sound of the poet's voice incorporating and extending the literal call of the oven bird. Or as Frost describes Eve in the garden of Eden listening to birds, she "added to their own an oversound." [13] This addition is human making, the invention of metaphor. (All poetic making is also making believe.) Metaphor is fabrication, a lie the poet builds in the name of the truth, and thus it contains the reality of what we add to what is there. Yet this making, enigmatic and uncertain, remains the only source of human belief. Such making is what Frost calls "real art . . . believing the thing into existence, saying as you go more than you even hoped you were going to be able to say." [14]

The season of fall is linked in "The Oven Bird" with the fall from the garden of Eden by the poetic act of naming: "And comes that other fall we name the fall." The poet has merged his voice with the oven bird, as Adam, in the book of *Genesis*, names the animals. So too the linking of literal meanings, speech, with poetic meanings, song, accomplishes the design by which the total poem exists in its own form and its own right. It is both sung prose and spoken song that enables Frost, as an oven bird, to know "in singing not to sing," for as speech can become song, and song can incorporate speech, as it does in this poem, so too can fact become metaphor, and metaphor, fact. These are the linkings that can constitute "felt truth." They are, made from enigma, the design of belief.

But belief is always grounded in the question out of which belief emerges. As the maker of belief, this is what Frost teaches and what the poet proclaims is the virtual effect of the bird's song which in reality is Frost's poem: "The question that he [both Frost and the oven bird] frames in all but words." The question is framed, just as the form of the sonnet constitutes a structural frame, and thus the question *implies* more than the words themselves can literally ask. The question embodies the *feeling* of the enigma of what man can make of himself and of his world. As Frost remarks in a letter to John Bartlett, "Remember that the sentence sound often says more than the words." [15] It is only because (like the bird song) the poem is framed, because it is a made thing, that the question it asks, and the answer of belief that it implies, can remain dynamically in tension. The poem remains open to the reader's own scrutiny. Such is the style of Frostian teaching.

The question asked by the oven bird is "what to make of a diminished thing." It comes at the end of the poem and thus it throws us back to the beginning, so that the poem makes a kind of circle. But the question, though specific enough, is also enigmatic: what "diminished thing?" Summer is a diminishing from spring, as the oven bird says, "as one to ten." Fall is a diminishing from summer. The fall from the garden of Eden is a mythical diminishing. Death, the highway "dust," is the diminishment of life. (What can one make of death?) The poem is a diminishing of the oven bird's loud call and its *possible* meanings. (All poetic form is made by choice and selection and thus a diminishing of nature's plenitude.) Aging on the highway, Frost too is a diminished thing. The poem itself, however, is the poet's only answer to these questions, for it is indeed what the poet has made. It is an order, a design, to set against uncertainty, to set against "the fall" and against death. As Frost asserts, "When in doubt there is always form for us to go on with." [16] And thus the reader is left with the enigma of what to make of the poem, a thing "diminished" into shape from the seeming chaos of life. Frost offers us a manmade form, and it is for us to be strengthened by it as such, to find in its own framed coherence what Frost himself believed to be there, "a momentary stay against confusion." [17] And those readers who actually have heard the call of an oven bird (or have looked it up in Roger Tory Peterson's *A Field Guide to the Birds*), will know that what the oven bird says is: "Teacher! Teacher!"

If the role of the poet-teacher is to make nature speak with a human voice, the role of the poet-preacher is to dramatize for the reader the mystery of divinity in the face of which belief must be given shape. In this role too, one finds the characteristic Frostian reserve:

> There may be little or much beyond the grave,
> But the strong are saying nothing until they see.[18]

Or, in a lighter mood:

> And I may return
> If dissatisfied
> With what I learn
> From having died.[19]

But Frost must speak, he must bear witness to the enigma of God in nature and offer his reader the story of that confrontation.

Frost describes a solitary man in his poem, "The Most of It," [20] who walks out to a "boulder-broken beach," repeatedly it seems, to "wake" a "voice" that would "answer" his "cry." It is as if there might be a God there who was unheeding, or asleep, who might respond to the man's call if properly summoned. In his naive wish, he is like the boy of Winander in Wordsworth's *The Prelude*,[21] who "both hands/ Pressed closely palm to palm," as if in unconscious prayer, "Blew mimic hootings to the silent owls,/ That they might answer him." But unlike Frost's man, Wordsworth's boy does receive a certain answer, and he does hear a voice speaking in the silence. The owls "shout again/ Responsive to his call," and then after they cease,

> in that silence while he hung
> Listening, a gentle shock of mild surprise
> Has carried far into his heart the voice
> Of mountain torrents.

What Frost's man receives is merely the "mocking echo of his own" voice, and so the narrator tells us "He thought he kept the universe alone." The man is literally alone, and alone in the deeper sense that he is without a God who is the keeper, the protector, of the universe. A man may keep promises, but the universe is more than he alone can keep or protect, more than he can keep watch over.

What the man cries out for, hoping to be heard, is not an echo or reminder of his own human love and human need, "But counterlove, original response." He wishes for God's love, "counter" to man's need, and God's "original" creative presence. Without God, man's world is only a boulder-broken beach, and man's voice calling out "on life," is a mockery of man's deepest desires. The narrator tells us that

> nothing ever came of what he cried
> Unless it was the embodiment that crashed
> In the cliff's talus.

The whole mystery of this poem hangs on the open word "unless," on what the man (and the reader) makes of that crashing embodiment. The poem's enigma is whether to regard that embodiment as a kind of incarnation or revelation, or merely as a physical phenomenon that has occurred "some morning" by chance. If it is seen as an incarnation of God's design, then it is indeed the "most of it," the most the man can wish for. It is revelation. If it is merely a physical event and not God's "voice in answer," it must be seen as the limiting "most" man can receive from nature. The design of nature, then, would be no more than the design of nature, alien to man.

The narrator describes the effect of the crashing embodiment literally, yet the impression the reader receives is uncertain and mysterious. There is a series of echoes. First, we hear the crash of loosening and tumbling stone. Then we hear the boulders splashing in the water. But what follows is a strange gap after which the boulders in the water *seem* to turn into a "great buck." The narrator says that this happens "after a time," as if it might be evolutionary time, as if the man has witnessed divine causality unfolding in a visionary instant. The narrator's difficult syntax suggests that it was the "embodiment" that "allowed" this transformation to take place. But even as the buck appears, it does not fulfill the man's expectation or hope. It is not seen as "original response," as "someone else additional to him." Described by the increasingly elusive word, "it," the buck is not regarded as the "most of it," although its natural power, like that of a "waterfall," is awesome. The question still remains: has the man witnessed more than a display of natural power?

What is the man, the narrator, the reader, to believe? The buck, with bountiful energy, "Pushing the crumpled water up ahead," seems to know what it is doing there, to have direction. But is this nature's random energy and force that "stumbled through the rocks," or is there the suggestion of a design that is to be read symbolically, as if life is to be seen here emerging from chaos and inorganic matter, pushing, landing, stumbling, forcing? The way the buck "forced the underbrush" resembles the way the image of the buck enters the sight and the mind of the man who is watching. That a powerful image is perceived is certain, but what can the mind make of that image, uniting rational thought with subconscious implications? It is as if the buck gets born in the mind of its perceiver. The narrator draws no conclusions, makes no assertions, and says flatly "that was all." But just as the title of the poem is firmly ambiguous in that "most" might mean everything the man hopes for, revelation, or merely the limit of what nature offers, so too is the last word, "all," ambiguous in the same way. Another voice echo occurs, "all" becomes an echo of "most." The phrase "that was all," therefore, with brilliant Frostian tonal irony, may imply disappointment, in that the man, hoping for a "voice in answer," sees only a buck, or "that was all" may suggest the man's jubilation in witnessing a gesture of divine revelation—all, everything—if the buck, though not what the man expected, is indeed regarded as an embodiment of God's presence in nature. The poem keeps these alternative possibilities clearly and absolutely in balance. The reader, like the man in the poem, is left to believe, if he will, one or the other, or perhaps, more accurately, he is left, knowing the extremes of possibility, unable to choose, confirmed only in his own uncertainty.

Can a man become "whole again beyond confusion?" [22] We see Frost again and again in his poems walking out into the darkness or venturing into an equivalent interior darkness, "To scare myself with my own desert places." [23] Frost's heroism is his refusal to avoid such confrontation or to escape into comforting dogma. In his sonnet, "Acquainted with the Night," [24] written in Dantean *terza rima*, Frost is in his own circle of hell, locked into an obsessive "I" of self-consciousness. The poem returns at the end to the line with which it begins, for there seems to be no way out of this circle. The speaker's movements outward in body or inward in thought both lead to the same darkness, the same "night." The "city light," and later the moon, the "luminary clock," paradoxically illuminate only this essential darkness, this absence of meaningful self-identity. We see the isolated speaker trying to walk beyond life itself to confront death, the ultimate isolation. In doing so, he detaches himself from the sorrow of human affairs as he looks back at the "saddest city lane," and feels what is perhaps a pang of guilt, as he passes "the watchman on his beat," for the extreme alienation he has perversely chosen. And so he drops his eyes, "unwilling to explain," even if he could, for he knows that the watchman is there to guard human lives and protect against the darkness, while he has elected to submerge himself in it.

How much death, how much isolation, can a man experience and still return to tell of it? When the speaker says, "I have stood still and stopped the sound of feet," the reader may feel that the speaker's heart has virtually stopped, or worse, that his spirit has died with his stilled body. That this is indeed spiritual death is suggested by the speaker's reaction to the anonymous "cry" that comes from the city of human suffering: the cry, he feels, has nothing to do with him, it does "not call me back or say goodbye." Having "outwalked the furthest city light," the speaker, in his imagination, journeys "further still," even beyond the world, to an "unearthly height," and envisions the moon as a clock. But time, the cosmos itself, is regarded as being without moral content and thus without meaning, it is "neither wrong nor right." In this sense, to live or to die also is neither wrong nor right, and to feel this way, in effect, is to be in hell. Such is the dark night that Frost confronts and finds within himself.

But the speaker does return, just as the poem returns to its first line. Close to death though he has come, he has not died, he has not experienced the ultimate isolation nor has he wrung from death its mystery. He says, having said it before, "I have been one acquainted with the night," and the reader knows that he has been, is, and will continue to be so acquainted. He will go on. He will, for a time, outwalk the death within him. He is "one," he feels himself to be alone, but such isolation is not equal to death itself. He still does not *know* death, he is merely *"acquainted* with the night." This is what he comes back to tell us. As far as a man may journey into darkness, he can never know it or discover what it ultimately may reveal. All he can know is that he is lost. With this paradoxical knowledge, he may begin his journey again, and if he is "lost enough to find [himself]," [25] he will go on trying to assert form, such as the circle this poem strategically makes, where there is darkness.

What every Frostian confrontation with nature teaches is that God's ways and His purpose for men are obscure, and the poet, as preacher, then must lead the reader to prayer without denying or sentimentalizing the divine mystery. Frost's courage is to live in doubt and yet still try to approach God through prayer. But as he says, "People should be careful how they pray. I've seen about as much harm as good come from prayer. It is highly doubtful if man is equipped for judicious prayer." [26] The paradox of "judicious prayer" is that it is not the result of reason, but of belief, and belief, for Frost, is always a made or invented thing. Frost, in the voice of God speaking to Job, says in "The Masque of Reason," "There's no connection man can reason out/ Between his just deserts and what he gets." [27] Frost must be the inventor of prayer, guiding his reader, in the hope that the human drive toward making form and order corresponds to something like a divine command to do so. And yet human order, the poem, must always acknowledge that in nature herself God's meaning is not to be discerned. The poet-preacher must teach his reader to pray that he be able to pray, he must teach him the absolute humility that man is not capable of judging his own works or his own worth. If there is a divine mercy, perhaps it is God's response to such humility. Or as Frost says in "A Masque of Mercy,"

> Our lives laid down in war and peace, may not
> Be found acceptable in Heaven's sight.
> And that they may be is the only prayer
> Worth praying.[28]

In "The Draft Horse," [29] an anonymous couple, like Adam and Eve late in the world's history, is seen, typically, on an unspecified journey. We do not know whether they are leaving home or returning home. They are in "too frail a buggy," suggesting the frailty of their bodies, and their lantern, suggesting their reason, sheds no light. It is "pitch-dark." Nothing can be seen. The narrative of the poem is enacted in this total darkness, so that, in effect, everything that takes place is imagined as in a nightmare vision. The grove through which the couple moves is "limitless." It would seem that there can be no end to their journey, no destination which might reveal the purpose and meaning of their travel's effort. Suddenly, a figure, described blankly as "a man," comes out of the woods and stabs their horse dead. His action is assumed to be deliberate, but for what intent and purpose, we do not know. Since the act occurs in absolute darkness, the reader can only assume that the speaker of the poem *assumes* that it is a man. It might as well be an angel or a devil or the speaker's own guilty fantasy. And, likewise, the assumption that this is a deliberate act is also enigmatic: has the man done this out of evil, merely to harm, or is there some purpose in the act, since it forces the couple to dismount and make their way through the dark entirely by the strength of their own spirits?

Having first been described as "too heavy a horse," the "beast" goes down "ponderous" with the weight of its own mortality. Everything weighs finally what death weighs. Death determines the measure of all things, and the "shaft," which seemingly gave the horse direction and purpose, is broken. If the "little horse" in "Stopping by Woods on a Snowy Evening" [30] shows an instinct to return home, not to remain in what the speaker feels to be the dangerously enticing woods, the heavy horse in this poem reveals only that this basic wish may be defeated. And just as the mysterious man has come "out of the trees," so too does the night

51

move "through the trees," as if the man and the night were the same or were directed by the same force. The night moves in an "invidious draft," enwrapping and destroying the "draft horse," so that their names merge, agent and victim become one, and all is reduced to a wind. The work of the draft horse has been completed, but nothing that the poem's speaker can reason out has been accomplished.

Can anything be made of this apparently meaningless and random event? The speaker describes himself and his companion as an "unquestioning pair." They are not, however, unthinking; they seem to know that knowledge has its limits in this "limitless grove," and, quite simply, they must accept this. They accept "fate" as a necessity, knowing that their freedom, if it exists at all, exists only in the attitude they take toward their fate, and thus the speaker says that they are

> . . . the least disposed to ascribe
> Any more than we had to to hate.

In their reluctance to respond to this event as the design of a malevolent force, a "design of darkness to appall," [31] they begin to define their own humanity. They will have to make something of this seemingly rebuking event that derives from their humanity, though they will never be certain that they are right to attribute this generosity to anything other than themselves. They will have only the fragile certainty of what belief provides. And yet the believer may speculate that this is precisely what God wants, precisely what His design demands: that man must respond to nature, and thus to God, out of man's own believing, not God's revelation. Therein is man's freedom. In this sense, it is the meaning that man makes out of unmeaning that reveals man in his greatest humanity. As God says to Job in "A Masque of Reason:"

> Too long I've owed you this apology
> For the apparently unmeaning sorrow
> You were afflicted with in those old days.
> But it was of the essence of the trial
> You shouldn't understand it at the time.
> It had to seem unmeaning to have meaning. [32]

The ability to make meaning of "apparently unmeaning sorrow" is synonymous with man's ability to pray. He must not pray *for* something; rather, he must *make* something and hope that—though this is never certain—the trial of that making will lead to his salvation, if not beyond the grave, at least within the measure of time.

And so, in "The Draft Horse," the couple makes what may be called a creative *assumption*. They choose to accept the apparently causeless punishment of fate, "let what will be, be," [33] as having a positive aspect. They assume that nature and human events must "obey" the laws of fate and that there is intent behind this design that must remain obscure to them. The man, that mysterious agent, no less than themselves, obeys the author of this design. The grove, the night, the wind, the man, the journeying couple—all are part of the design. And the only free act that the couple can perform is to "assume" that there is meaning in this enigmatical design. The closest Frost comes to naming God in this poem is when he refers to "someone [the man] had to obey," but surely an unknowable God is there by implication. What this obscure, controlling force demands, or so the couple chooses to assume, is only that they must "get down/ And walk the rest of the way." Why this "someone" wants this, they are not told, and they do not know. Just as the grove is limitless, so too are the possible explanations for what the couple has experienced and what the reader has been given to witness. Although reason cannot unravel the mystery here, Frost's parable is rich with implications which he, as preacher-poet, has locked into the poem with firm intent. Again, for Frost, the poem itself resists the darkness which it confronts, both as a manmade order and as an assumption that the outer darkness, the cosmos, is also an order, and as such may be believed to contain a benevolent intent. This is the inherent prayer the poem makes and invites the reader to participate in. And so to this darkness the poet must unceasingly turn, for it is the source of all that he is and all that he may become:

> The background is hugeness and confusion shading away from where we stand into black and utter chaos; and against the background any small man-made figure of order and concentration. What pleasanter than that it should be so? . . . This confusion . . . we like it, we were born to it, born used to it and have practical reasons for wanting it there. To me any little form I assert upon it is velvet, as the saying is, and to be considered for how much more it is than nothing.[34]

Perhaps, then, the reader himself may assume that there is indeed good in the couple having to "walk the rest of the way," having to be entirely on their own. They are compelled to make of "the way" what they can and what they will, just as the poet has made the poem out of darkness, out of "nothing." Where the "way" will lead to, the poem does not tell us, but as Frost says, "The one inalienable right is to go to destruction in your own way. What's worth living for is worth dying for." [35] What lies beyond the grave the strong do not venture to guess at. There may be nothing, and that enigma remains part of the darkness in which we live. But if Frost as teacher, preacher, and poet, "acquainted with the night," [36] is to keep going along the way, and is to be true to the God he believes in but does not know, he must imitate his enigmatical creator, he must maintain his own "proper enigmatical reserve" in the making of his poems.

NOTES

[1] Robert Frost quoted in Lawrance Thompson, *Robert Frost, The Years of Triumph, 1915–1938* (New York: Holt, Rinehart and Winston, 1970), p. 250.

[2] Lawrance Thompson, *Robert Frost, The Early Years, 1874–1915* (New York: Holt, Rinehart and Winston, 1966), p. 578.

[3] Robert Frost, *Selected Prose*, ed. Hyde Cox and Edward Connery Lathem (New York: Collier Books, 1968), p. 114.

[4] Robert Frost, *Complete Poems* (New York: Henry Holt and Company, 1959), p. 131.

[5] Thompson, *The Early Years*, p. 546.

[6] Robert Frost, *In the Clearing* (New York: Holt, Rinehart and Winston, 1962), p. 39.

[7] Frost, *Complete Poems*, p. 126.

[8] Ibid., p. 139.

[9] Ibid., p. 150.

[10] Reuben Brower, *The Poetry of Robert Frost* (New York: Oxford University Press, 1968), p. 31.

[11] Ralph Waldo Emerson, *Selections*, ed. Stephen E. Whicher (Boston: Houghton Mifflin Company, 1960), p. 263.

[12] Frost, *Selected Prose*, p. 115.

[13] Frost, *Complete Poems*, p. 452.

[14] Frost, *Selected Prose*, p. 46.

[15] Elaine Barry, *Robert Frost on Writing* (New Brunswick, N.J.: Rutgers University Press, 1973), p. 66.

[16] Frost, *Selected Prose*, p. 106.

[17] Ibid., p. 18.

[18] Frost, *Complete Poems*, p. 391.

[19] Frost, *In the Clearing*, p. 15.

[20] Frost, *Complete Poems*, p. 451.

[21] William Wordsworth, *The Prelude*, ed. Ernest de Selincourt (New York: Oxford University Press, 1950), pp. 155, 157.

[22] Frost, *Complete Poems*, p. 521.

[23] Ibid., p. 586.

[24] Ibid., p. 324.

[25] Ibid., p. 521.

[26] Thompson, *The Early Years*, pp. 673–74.

[27] Frost, *Complete Poems*, p. 589.

[28] Ibid., p. 642.

[29] Frost, *In the Clearing*, p. 60.

[30] Frost, *Complete Poems*, p. 275.

[31] Ibid., p. 396.

[32] Ibid., p. 589.

[33] Ibid., p. 313.

[34] Frost, *Selected Prose*, p. 107.

[35] Ibid., p. 116.

[36] Frost, *Complete Poems*, p. 324.

It goes without saying that Allen Tate scarcely needs an introduction here. At the Library of Congress he is a most welcome presence, for some 30 years ago he held the Consultantship in Poetry. He not only lent that post the distinction of his presence but left behind him an invaluable bibliography, published by the Library, of the 60 leading American poets of the 1940's, and the first tapes in our Archive of Recorded Poetry. This last project is one the continuation of which has become one of the chief and most pleasant responsibilities of succeeding poetry consultants.

Mr. Tate is the inevitable speaker to conclude our series of lectures honoring the centenary of Robert Frost today, not only because he was born in the same century as the older poet whom we honor, but also because Allen Tate is the First Citizen in our Republic of Letters. From the time his first book of verse, Mr. Pope and Other Poems, *appeared in 1928, until now —45 years, and nearly as many books, later—his preeminence as both poet and interpreter of literature has been a happy fact of this country's cultural life. First as a spokesman for his native region, then as a distinguished practitioner of the twin arts of poetry and criticism, Mr. Tate has both embodied in his poems the values of our literature and, in his essays, showed us what to regard as, and how to respond to, the best in our heritage of culture, literature, and the very language we use.*

I infer from his title that he will reveal an aspect of Frost we have scarcely suspected but will be much rewarded by having him point out to us.

~⸘

"Inner Weather"
ROBERT FROST AS METAPHYSICAL POET

by Allen Tate

ROBERT FROST, "like other poets who have written with narrow views, and paid court to temporary prejudices, has been at one time too much praised, and too much neglected at another." I have substituted Robert Frost for Abraham Cowley in this quotation from Samuel Johnson's *Life of Cowley*; the sentence introduces the critical discussion of Cowley's poems and of certain other poets whom Johnson mistakenly called "metaphysical," as mistakenly as I have called Frost a metaphysical poet. Everybody knows that Johnson meant by "metaphysical" something like abstruse, complex, difficult. But so is Robert Frost difficult, in his own way. What looks like simplicity will turn out to be—or so my reading of him tells me—mere simplicity at the surface, below which lies a *selva oscura* that I shall be able to point to without quite getting inside it. And I must say here at the outset that I am not alluding to Mr. Lionel Trilling's famous 85th-birthday speech, even though I agree with it. It was the first critical effort to break through the Chinese Wall of Frostian adulation. Although I am aware that I am beginning with the negative side of my observations on Robert Frost, I must go a little further and confess that Frost was not, when I was a young man, my kind of poet; nor is he now that I am an old man; and yet I am convinced that he wrote some of the finest poems of our time, or of any time. The Earl of Rochester wrote some of the best short poems in the language, but he is not my kind of poet. I am not linking Rochester and Frost; I am merely saying that one may admire what is not entirely sympathetic, and by not sympathetic I could mean that perhaps the poet wouldn't unreservedly like me.

Now, 11 years after his death, Frost is in partial eclipse. And nine years after his death, T. S. Eliot is equally in the penumbra of a declining reputation. One expects this immediately after the death of a famous writer. One wonders whether an occasion, such as this centenary celebration, will restore some of the popularity that Robert Frost enjoyed for almost 50 years. Is the living voice, back of the printed line, necessary? During his lifetime his readers could see, synesthetically, back of the poems they were reading, the handsome, massive face of the master and the dramatic changes of expression. Without the living presence one attends more closely to what is said and how Frost says it. For Johnson's phrase "narrow views" I would substitute monotonous metrics and a monotony of tone which results from a narrowly calculated vocabulary. In this he resembles Housman or even John Clare, but the resemblance is only superficial. I don't want the old gentleman to turn over in his grave; and yet I must risk it when I agree with Herbert Howarth that Frost was a reformer of poetic diction, contemporaneous with Ford Madox Ford, Pound, and Eliot, and that the necessity of reform was as plain to him, even if the result was different, as it was to his younger contemporaries. I shall return to this matter after a personal digression which I hope the audience will allow me.

At the end of September 1928 I had arrived in London as a Guggenheim Fellow. I met in the first week a few English writers through the kindness of T. S. Eliot and Herbert Read. I don't remember whether the invitation came from Read or Eliot; at any rate an emissary, Frank Morley, a man my age, came for me in Kensington Garden Square to escort me to my first "Criterion Luncheon" at a pub whose name I forget. (After lunch Morley took me on a "pub crawl"—which may explain my faulty memory of that first meeting with Eliot and Read, with whom I had had previous correspondence.) After my second or third Criterion Luncheon I received an invitation from Harold Monro (whom I had not met) to come to a party at his flat above the famous Poetry Bookshop at 38 Great Russell Street. I do not remember the exact date in October; I don't think it could have been a party given after Robert Frost's reading on the 18th at the Poetry Bookshop, nor on the 19th, after Monro had brought Frost and Eliot together at dinner, for at the party I attended there were 10 or 12 people present, but not Eliot. I remember vividly Frank Flint—F. S. Flint, the prominent Imagist now forgotten by everybody but literary historians. Herbert Read soon came to talk to me and then took me to the other end of the room (near a grate fire) where a circle of men were listening to an animated monolog. The circle broke, and I was introduced to "Mr. Robert Frost." He turned to face me, and we shook hands. We talked a little, about what I don't remember, but he asked me where I was from; I think I said Kentucky and Virginia. And he said to the company—which included, besides those I have mentioned, A. W. Wheen, Lascelles Abercrombie, Richard Church—he said, "Tate's vowels are different from mine. Just listen. 'The murmurous haunt of flies on summer eves.' Won't you repeat it," he said to me. I did, and he said to the company, "There's the difference between New England and the South." But he then said to me, "Your consonants are too distinct for a Southerner." That's all I remember except the small, sharp eyes, the noble brow, the fine, rugged features, and the dignified bearing. I had read very few of his poems, but I knew then that I was in the presence of a great man. I didn't see him again until 19 years later.

In the commentary that follows—it will be my tribute to the genius of Robert Frost—I shall try to talk about the poems I consider the best, regardless of subject or the time of his life in which they were written. Beginning with *North of Boston* in 1914 and ending with *In the Clearing* (1962), when he was 88, there is a uniformity of style that, with few exceptions, would make it difficult to date most of the poems. (*A Boy's Will*, his first book, shows influences not of any identifiable poets but of the period: American Edwardian or Georgian.) The uniformity of diction has been called Wordsworthian; but with Frost it is difficult to determine whether theory, as in the case of Wordsworth, or a sure instinct for what he could best do, explains the monotony of consciously simplified diction and the prevailing iambic pentameter in both the meditative and the narrative poems. With the exceptions of the two masques, all his characters talk alike, with only an occasional departure from the simple but correct speech of the "literate farmer." One merely observes, without trying to explain, the comparative inferiority of the more "lyrical" poems, such as "To Earthward," "An Empty Threat," "I Will Sing you One, O," and half a dozen others. One's observation, however, may include the opinion that Robert Frost was not a first-rate lyric poet, for in this genre he "sings" less than he merely ruminates, as he does at the end of "To Earthward" or "The Aim Was Song." And the short, political epigrams that he wrote late in life—who will hold them against him?

In more than 50 years of writing he published about 560 poems, some long, others no more than a few lines. How many did he discard, unpublished? No poet so prolific as Robert Frost could expect to write more good poems than he wrote. Those that I shall comment on may seem to the Frost devotée an ungenerous, even perverse selection. Are not all the works of the master sacrosanct? If he has written one great poem, even a very short one, all the others must be considered. To my way of looking at poetry, he wrote more than one great—I shall not say lyric—more than one great short poem, and perhaps a dozen longer pieces. I don't know what else to call the longer poems. They are either meditations or short stories in verse, usually in iambic pentameter and always, whatever the meter and foot, metrical: there is always the tennis net. As to the shorter pieces, he never wrote anything as bad as Shakespeare's Sonnet LXXXV or as great as Sonnet LXXIII; not a bad rating, for those interested in ratings, for any poet since 1616. And although his scene is almost always "country things," I cannot see him with Mr. John F. Lynen as a pastoral poet (*The Pastoral Art of Robert Frost*, 1960). I can find neither prelapsarian shepherds nor abstract sheep. There is nothing resembling either the *Idyls* of Theocritus or the *Eclogues* of Vergil. We know that Frost's Latin was fluent, and his Greek adequate, and his command of both languages probably better than Ezra Pound's more ostentatious exhibits. But Frost seems to me to have been too canny to write eclogues and idyls, even though his dialogs may have been suggested by his early reading of Vergil and Theocritus.

Before we pass on from this phase of Frost I should like to look rather closely at what I consider his finest longer—not very long or longest—poem: "The Witch of Coös." A month ago, or a few months hence, I might prefer the shorter "The Wood-Pile" or "West-Running Brook"; for with a poet who wrote so many fine poems, choice becomes uncertain and difficult. I am thinking of "The Witch of Coös" because it is typical of Frost's whimsical preference for the shocking circumstance that lies hidden beneath a conventional human situation. Like every first-rate work of art—poem, picture, sculpture, film—it invites endlessly varied interpretations, and all of them may be "right." I wish to look at "The Witch of Coös" through the eyes of Henry James—if I may commit a double presumption, even impertinence. To the question of what makes the skeleton in the poem fictionally real, there may be several answers. I assume that everybody knows the plot, but I shall have to repeat it in outline. The scene is set in the three opening lines:

> I stayed the night for shelter at a farm
> Behind the mountain, with a mother and son,
> Two old-believers. They did all the talking.

This is not quite plausible. Why should the mother tell her dreadful secret to a stranger, whom the poet makes no effort to establish as a character? Why did Henry James let the governess in *The Turn of the Screw* write her horrid story for nobody in particular, although in the prolog James explains how her manuscript got into the hands of his host at an English country house? A fiction must be told to somebody, if it aims at the highest plausibility; otherwise, as in the primitive novel, the novelist is merely listening to the sound of his own voice, as Thackeray, a sophisticated Londoner, is doing in his unsophisticated novel *Vanity Fair*. In "The Witch of Coös," the wayfaring stranger, in the three lines that I have quoted, not only sets the scene in a remote place—"behind the mountain"—he tells us that both mother and son are "old-believers"—hindsight some time after the action to prepare us for something, an incident, an unusual natural phenomenon, or some discredited superstition, to which he will be the witness. I say "witness" because he not only hears, he *sees* up to the limit that language will permit us to see, and it is not fictionally necessary to know whether this shadowy reporter actually believes what he hears and sees.

But let me dispose at once of the single flaw that I can find in an otherwise almost perfect work; I say almost because no work of art is perfect. It was not at all necessary to make the mother a spirit-medium, a table-rapper who can make the table kick "like an army mule." The action begins when the son asks his mother

> You wouldn't want to tell him what we have
> Up in the attic . . . ?

And she replies:

> Bones—a skeleton.

This "dreadfully" complex poem is, amusingly enough, a marvelous development of the common saying that we all have a skeleton in the closet. What appears to have happened is this: the mother had committed adultery with a man whom her husband killed, she says, "instead of me."[1] They bury the corpse in the cellar. Her relation to her husband is frigid. She says:

> I went to sleep before I went to bed,
> Especially in winter when the bed
> Might just as well be ice and the clothes snow.

The bones come up the cellar stairs, "two footsteps for each step." Her curiosity is so great that she waits for him to see "how they were mounted for this walk." The skeleton stretched out its hand and she struck it, breaking it off, and she keeps a finger in her "button box." The common details by which the bones are made credible are the selection of a master; we are not allowed to see too much, or even very much. Frost instinctively found himself among the masters of credibility for the supernatural—Henry James and W. W. Jacobs. Whether the supernatural be hallucinatory or what it purports to be, need not concern us here. Let us glance at the way the woman sees the bones (as she always speaks of them), for that is the way Frost will let us see them. The "bones" emerge from the cellar; she envisions "them put together/ Not like a man, but like a chandelier". And then:

> Still going every which way in the joints, though,
> So that it looked like lightning or a scribble,
> From the slap I had just now given its hand.

She calls upstairs to her husband to get up, and she follows the bones to their bedroom, where she admits to her husband, whose curious name is Toffile, that she can't see the bones, but insists that they want to go up to the attic, which they do without being seen by her husband, or seen a second time by her. Toffile is ordered by his wife to get nails and nail up the door to the attic where the bones have presumably fled; and Toffile pushed the headboard of their bed against the attic door.

> Behind the door and headboard of the bed,
> Brushing their chalky skull with chalky fingers,
> With sounds like the dry rattling of a shutter,
> That's what I sit up in the dark to say—
> To no one anymore since Toffile died.
> Let them stay in the attic since they went there.

I promised Toffile to be cruel to them
For helping them be cruel once to him.

The wayfaring stranger has the last word:

She hadn't found the finger-bone she wanted
Among the buttons poured out in her lap.
I verified the name next morning: Toffile.
The rural letter box said Toffile Lajway.

James would not have let her find it; nor would Jacobs in his masterpiece "The Monkey's Paw." You will remember that great story. The son of an elderly couple is dead, but they are promised his return from the grave. He does return, as far as the front door where his parents are waiting to receive him. But they never see him. The story ends with the psychic shock resulting from having heard a walking corpse, without actually seeing it.

Is the widow a witch because she alone, *when alone*, could see the bones and snatch a finger? There is no indication that she saw them again. Are they merely the "dry rattling of a shutter?" We shall never know, and I submit that Frost's little masterpiece would be ruined if we could know. Canny old Robert might himself have told us that he didn't know. At any rate, what James said in the preface to *The Aspern Papers* is a rule that Frost's genius knew without James' help. Apparitions, said James, should do as little as is consistent with their consenting to appear at all.

Frost's most popular poems are little short stories in verse, a feature observed by many critics, preeminently by W. W. Robson, whose essay in the autumn 1966 issue of *The Southern Review* seems to me the best short study of Frost that we have. I would amend Robson's perception: short story to anecdote. I would cite a few famous poems that seem to me to be brilliant anecdotes. An anecdote differs from a short story in having a simple plot, or a single incident, in which there is no change of character. Even "The Witch of Coös" is an elaborated anecdote. The most obvious of Robert Frost's anecdotes is "The Death of the Hired Man" (it is not only obvious; it is one of the best of its genre). The old man comes back to work, and he is a skilled hay-pitcher. Warren, the farmer-employer, doesn't want to take him back, but his wife insists. So Warren goes back to the old man, returns to his wife to report him dead, and the poem ends. The anecdote is "used," the old, dying hired man is "used," to create a quasi-dramatic situation for two opposing epigrams about the nature of a home. Warren's:

> Home is the place where, when you have to go there,
> They have to take you in.

Mary's:

> I should have called it
> Something you somehow haven't to deserve.

There is always with us the famous "Birches," a poem that I am
fond of with the least possible admiration—the way we sometimes
feel about certain old friends. Not that it isn't beautifully written.
I don't remember ever mentioning it in print, but I must have
long ago, for Mr. Radcliffe Squires says that I consider it an allegory of the poet (*The Major Themes of Robert Frost*, 1963). Poets
are like swingers of birches, for they too are engaged upon a profit-
less enterprise. "That would be good both going and coming back":
it is good to write the poem (this is the upswing), and it is good
to see it finished (this is the downswing). I have felt for a long
time that "Marse Robert" might have spared us the sententious
meiosis of the last line. Do I need to quote it? I will quote it: "One
could do worse than be a swinger of birches." Yes, of course; but
unless they are symbolic birches (in an Emersonian direction), if
they are just plain birches, one could talk back and say that one
could do a lot better than be a swinger of birches. The birches seem
too frail to bear such a portentous allegory.

And now the famous wall that has a fine, domestic, and civic
effect upon the people it divides. Either wall or fence. Alas, *something* can neither like nor dislike a wall—unless Frost is saying
that mystery shrouds the human resistance to confinement, or
perimeters, of any kind; and he observes nature's harsh treatment
of walls and fences; the stones must be put up again, year after year,
as the two characters in the poem are doing. This is the action to
which their dialog about fences is the accompaniment. Nobody likes
walls or fences, but if we are going to live near one another, if
we are going to have even the first bare rudiment of a civilized
society, we had better do something to preserve the privacy of the
family, like putting up a fence or a wall; otherwise we will find
ourselves living atavistically in a tribal society. I hope my rather
feckless paraphrase of this poem is at least as tiresome as the poem
itself. I have a little more to say about it. Good neighbors are good
to have, but good fences do not make them good neighbors. Here
we have Frost's perilous teetering upon the brink of sentimentality.
Fences good or bad make nothing; but upon the rhetorical trick

64

that attributes causation to them the poem depends. I could wish that this fine poet had drawn upon his classical learning and had alluded to the first thing the Romans did when they were making a settlement: they built a low wall that would enclose a forum and in the middle set up an altar. The wall around the altar shut out the Infinite, or as the Greeks said it, το ἄπειρον, as if they might have foreseen the disorderly love of infinity that Walt Whitman would bring into the world. May I suggest that Frost's limited perspective in this poem is due to what I have called (after Samuel Johnson) his "narrow views." The views are not only opinions but the deliberate restriction of his language to the range possible to that ghostly, hypothetical person, the "literate farmer." Short range of consciousness means limited diction. I shall have more to say about this in a moment.

I cannot do much about a list of very fine poems which there is no time to discuss in detail. "The White-Tailed Hornet," "Place for a Third," "A Star in a Stone Boat," "Two Tramps in Mud Time," "Fear," "Once by the Pacific," "After Apple-Picking." One tires of making lists. Tomorrow I might make another list equally distinguished, attaching to it a list of neutral poems that exhibit the defect of Frost's quality. So I shall now indulge in what will look like a digression, and may actually be a digression, which was suggested by Mr. Howarth's valuable essay in the Frost symposium in the autumn 1966 issue of *The Southern Review*. He is, I believe, the only critic to see in Frost's restricted diction a revolutionary reform contemporaneous with the experiments in poetic diction of Pound and Eliot. Pound, in England, was Frost's first champion, but Frost would not follow Pound into an international, eclectic, and "learned" style. (Is this the meaning of Frost's "The Road Not Taken"? Perhaps.) At any rate Frost must have believed that in order to break new stylistic ground he had to *locate it literally*. It was inevitable that he would locate it in New England. Half Scottish, half New Englander, he was taken by his widowed mother from San Francisco to New England when he was 11. He had the ideal upbringing for a poet, and it is irrelevant that he disliked it. He was half in and half out, and he could take nothing for granted. Thus his powers of observation, which were great, led to equally great gifts for discovery: he saw New England nature and the nature of New England man as his own, but both natures had to be discovered. He therefore invented a language for this double imaginative activity. He was much more the conscious technician than some of his critics have thought. Did he not write to his friend John Bartlett that he was one of the great craftsmen? There is nothing reprehensible in this kind of boasting if it is true; and this was.

For many years I have argued with skeptics that the Eliot-Pound revolution was as radical as that brought about by two other young men in 1798—or rather by one of them, William Wordsworth. In the famous Preface to the 1800 edition of *Lyrical Ballads*, Wordsworth said that he wanted to write in the "real language of men." Which men? Rural men was the answer, and he wrote a masterpiece called "Michael." But Frost's "literate farmer" never gave utterance to such absurdities as "Peter Bell" and "The Idiot Boy"; nor did he ever, as Mr. Robson points out, achieve the grandeur of "Resolution and Independence." Wordsworth broke out of his early mould; Robert Frost did not. Yet in certain respects Frost was subtler and a more sensitive listener to the sounds of poetry. He anticipated by many years T. S. Eliot's discovery of the "auditory imagination." Frost called it the audile (or audial) imagination, and he described it as the "sound of the meaning"—a very different effect from that which Pope had in mind when he wrote that "The sound must seem to echo in the sense." I take it that Frost would have said that there is no meaning to be sounded in a line like "The Hounds of Spring are on winter's traces," etc.

As I approach the end of these scattered observations I allude to three or four poems that seem to me Robert Frost's best: "The Wood-Pile," which ends with the great line "With the slow smokeless burning of decay"; "After Apple-Picking"; "The Onset"; and "The Oven Bird." But where is "Stopping by Woods on a Snowy Evening?" Had Frost written this one short masterpiece, and no others, his name would last as long as poetry itself will last. (We cannot assume that even poetry will last forever.) Here it is:

> Whose woods these are I think I know.
> His house is in the village, though;
> He will not see me stopping here
> To watch his woods fill up with snow.
>
> My little horse may think it queer
> To stop without a farmhouse near
> Between the woods and frozen lake
> The darkest evening of the year.

He gives his harness bells a shake
To ask if there is some mistake.
The only other sound's the sweep
Of easy wind and downy flake.

The woods are lovely, dark, and deep,
But I have promises to keep,
And miles to go before I sleep,
And miles to go before I sleep.

It has the rhyme scheme of Fitzgerald's *Rubaiyat* stanza: *a a b a*. But the meter is tetrameter, not, as in the *Rubaiyat*, pentameter. The four stanzas are "linked" in much the same way as Dante's *terzine* are linked. The unrhymed "here" in the first stanza is rhymed with the two first lines and with the fourth of the second, and so on, until we get to the last stanza, in which the third line rhymes with two and four; in short, one rhyme only in that stanza, as one will repeat a phrase, or see oneself walking in a dream, or as one drifts off into sleep. These formalistic external features of the poem have scarcely been noticed; they contribute to the overwhelming, if quiet, effect. Here our literate farmer is, in the very first line, highly sophisticated. It contains both a question and the answer to the question: "Whose woods are these?" And in the same grammatical sequence: "I think I know." But the owner is in town, and he will not see me observe the recurrent mystery of winter, which is snow. We are not told that the man watching the snowfall is in a sleigh. The horse knows that something unusual is happening, though not to the eye, his or his master's. There is no house nearby; the man is isolated in the "darkest evening," his own darkness. The "harness bells" add a dimension of sound to the sibilance of the blowing snow. The lake is frozen; the usually beneficent water is obdurate, and nature has withdrawn her protection. The fourth stanza has all the appearance of the calculation of genius. But Frost told a friend that the entire poem came to him in a flash, or rather phrase by phrase, rhyme scheme and meter, without a pause. There is every reason to believe him. The external pattern reflects perfectly what we are told; instead of the third unrhymed line, as in the three other stanzas, there is, as I have said, one rhyme: deep-keep-sleep-sleep. As one falls asleep it takes too much effort to find a rhyme; so sleep echoes sleep. We may see here what Mr. Cleanth Brooks formerly saw as a paradox: the poet falls asleep as he tells us that he will not. But the most brilliant single word in the poem is that common word "lovely." Years ago I almost dismissed the poem because "lovely" struck me as a lazy evasion of the precise word. But it *is* the precise word. The woods are a lovely woman, but a woman cold, mysterious (dark), and unfathomable, and he must not succumb to this temptress, who is both life and death. Frost thought of the poem as a "death poem." As I see it, it has as much of life in it as any poem of the same length in the language. It could hold its own with the great lyric of the 19th century, "Tears, Idle Tears."

In the spring of 1961 Robert Frost came to Minneapolis to give a reading at the University of Minnesota. I was asked to introduce him, which I took great pleasure in doing, to a packed auditorium of 5,000 persons. He was the houseguest of a colleague of mine, Charles Foster, a former student of Frost's at Amherst. Frost was with us almost a week. I had two parties for him. At the second party, at about two in the morning, after all the guests except the Fosters had gone home, he asked for another brandy. I brought it to him, though I could hardly stand up, not from intoxication but from fatigue. He was then 87.

On January 5, 1963, I was at Yale, in the library, as a member of the jury for the Bollingen Prize of 1962. Up to that time the Bollingen juries tacitly assumed that to award Robert Frost the prize would carry coals to Newcastle. But in 1963 we knew he was dying in a Boston hospital. There was no time left for him to get the Nobel Prize. The jury—composed of Robert Lowell, John Hall Wheelock, Richard Eberhart, the late Louise Bogan, and myself—voted unanimously to award him the prize. Would he accept it? I was appointed to telephone him and ask. I did; his feeble voice came through distinctly. "Is this Allen?" he said. I said, "Yes, and we hope you will accept the Bollingen Prize for 1962." After a brief silence he said, "I've wondered where you fellows stood."

NOTES

[1] Who killed the witch's lover? Her husband, it is now plain to me, after an error of many years in assuming that *his* father did it. The passage is tricky, but obviously the husband was the murderer. After this essay was read at the Library of Congress on March 26, 1974, Mr. Daniel Hoffman and Mr. William Meredith informed me of my mistake. I am grateful to both.

The program of the evening dramatic performance is reproduced here to complete the record.

THE GERTRUDE CLARKE WHITTALL POETRY AND LITERATURE FUND

By Arrangement with

MATINEE THEATRE SERIES

A project of the
White Barn Theatre Foundation, Inc.
LUCILLE LORTEL, Artistic Director

Presents

The Open Eye Company
JEAN ERDMAN, Artistic Director

in

ROBERT FROST, WITH RHYME AND REASON

lighting design   stage manager
George Gracey   Tony Davis

PART I: "RHYMES"
poems of Robert Frost
arranged & directed by John Genke
songs composed & sung by Wendy Erdman
music by Teiji Ito & Dan Erkkila
"The Silken Tent" choreographed by Jean Erdman
poems spoken by John FitzGibbon, John Genke & Lee McClelland

The Road Not Taken ....John FitzGibbon
To The Thawing Wind ....Company
Blue-Butterfly Day ....Lee McClelland
Fragmentary Blue ....John Genke, Lee McClelland
The Telephone ....John FitzGibbon, Lee McClelland
Nothing Gold Can Stay ....John Genke
Tree at My Window ....Wendy Erdman
The Death of the Hired Man ....John FitzGibbon, Lee McClelland
Lines Written in Dejection on the Eve of Great Success .....Wendy Erdman
A Time To Talk ....John FitzGibbon
Not All There ....John Genke
Lodged ....Lee McClelland
A Reflex ....Company
Any Size We Please ....John Genke
The Pasture ....John FitzGibbon
The Silken Tent ....Danced by Jean Erdman
Spoken by John Genke
To Earthward ....Lee McClelland
The Subverted Flower ....John Genke
Wind And Window Flower ....Wendy Erdman
Home Burial ....John FitzGibbon, John Genke, Lee McClelland
Fire And Ice ....Wendy Erdman
I Could Give All to Time ....John Genke
Come In ....Lee McClelland
After Apple-Picking ....John FitzGibbon
Stopping by Woods on a Snowy Evening ....Wendy Erdman

—Intermission—

PART II: "A MASQUE OF REASON"
by Robert Frost

Scene: A fair oasis in the purest desert.

Job ....John Genke
Thyatira, his wife ....Lee McClelland
God ....John FitzGibbon
Satan ....Dan Erkkila

Directed by
Albert Takazauckas

From THE POETRY OF ROBERT FROST, Edited by Edward Connery
Lathem. Copyright 1969 by Holt, Rinehart and Winston, Inc.
Grateful acknowledgment is made to the Publishers for permission to use these
poems in musical settings at The Library of Congress, Washington, D. C.

THE COMPANY

THE OPEN EYE, founded by choreographer Jean Erdman and author Joseph
Campbell, has developed an unusual ensemble of creative and performing
artists. Each was engaged initially for roles in the highly successful first

oduction, "Moon Mysteries," an interpretation of three visionary plays by
. B. Yeats, conceived and directed by Miss Erdman. From varied careers
the theater, music, and dance, these artists have now joined as permanent
embers of this new performing unit, combining their talents in the produc-
on of works fusing music, plot, and visual image. Those participating in
is evening's "Robert Frost, With Rhyme And Reason" are:

Actors

)HN FITZGIBBON, an Obie nominee last season for his performance in
The Cat And The Moon," last appeared on Broadway in "The Incomparable
ax!" Off-Broadway he was seen as Ted Ken O'Dunc in "Macbird" and Pierre
"The Screens."

)HN GENKE has acted with both the American and New York Shakespeare
estivals as well as off-Broadway and in Regional Theater. Roles have in-
uded Macbeth, Vladimir in "Waiting For Godot" and Bob Acres in "The
ivals." This is his directing debut.

EE McCLELLAND appeared off-Broadway in "The House of Bernarda
lba" and "The Respectful Prostitute." In three seasons at Monmouth, Maine
ie has played such Shakespeare heroines as Juliet, Rosalind, Isabella in
Measure for Measure" and Hermione in "The Winter's Tale."

Musicians

'ENDY ERDMAN sings both classical and folk music and has recorded an
bum of her own songs, "Erdman" (Audio Fidelity). Recently, she com-
)sed a score for "Mandragola" and sang the role of Anna in the world
remiere of "The Play of Mary" in New York.

)AN ERKKILA, an orchestra and chamber musician as well as soloist, com-
)sed music for the NBC special "The Unexplained" and has also created
veral dance scores. He worked with Teiji Ito on "Watermill' for the New
ork City Ballet.

'EIJI ITO composed the score for Jerome Robbins' "Watermill." He received
1 Obie award for his music for "Three Modern Japanese Plays," and has
so created scores for the Living Theater's "In the Jungle of Cities" and
:an Erdman's "Coach With the Six Insides."

Dancer

EAN ERDMAN, the Artistic Director of the Open Eye, received the Vernon
ice and Obie Awards for her play, "The Coach With the Six Insides," and
as given a Drama Desk Award and a Tony Nomination for her chore-
graphy in the Broadway hit "Two Gentlemen of Verona."

Director

LBERT TAKAZAUCKAS has directed such diverse plays as "Troilus and
ressida," "Pal Joey," and Checkov's "Plotonov." In addition, he has staged
peras by Mozart, Handel, Hindemith, and the world premiere of Joyce
arthelson's "The King's Breakfast" for the National Federation of Music.

Costume Designer

1ICHAEL MASSEE designed the costumes for "A Masque of Reason."

OTHER PUBLICATIONS ON LITERATURE
ISSUED BY THE
LIBRARY OF CONGRESS

Unless otherwise noted, these publications, based on lectures presented at the Library of Congress, may be purchased from the Superintendent of Documents, Government Printing Office, Washington, D.C. 20402. When ordering, please provide the title, date, and identifying number, and enclose payment.

American Poetry at Mid-Century. 1958. 49 p. Reprinted in *Literary Lectures.*
  New Poets and Old Muses, by John Crowe Ransom. The Present State of Poetry, by Delmore Schwartz. The Two Knowledges, by John Hall Wheelock.

Anni Mirabiles, 1921-1925: Reason in the Madness of Letters, by Richard P. Blackmur. 1956. 55 p. Reprinted in *Literary Lectures.*
  The Great Grasp of Unreason. The Techniques of Trouble. Irregular Metaphysics. Contemplation.

Anniversary Lectures, 1959. 1959. 56 p. LC 29.9:H55. 75 cents. Also reprinted in *Literary Lectures.*
  Robert Burns, by Robert S. Hillyer. The House of Poe, by Richard Wilbur. Alfred Edward Housman, by Cleanth Brooks.

The Art of History. Two Lectures. 1967. 38 p. LC 29.9:N41. 60 cents.
  The Old History and the New, by Allan Nevins. Biography, History, and the Writing of Books, by Catherine Drinker Bowen.

Carl Sandburg, by Mark Van Doren. With a bibliography of Sandburg materials in the collections of the Library of Congress. 1969. 83 p. LC 29.9:V28. $1.00.

Chaos and Control in Poetry; a Lecture, by Stephen Spender. 1966. 14 p. LC 29.9:SP3/2. 55 cents.

Dante Alighieri. Three Lectures. 1965. 53 p. Out of print.
  The Interest in Dante Shown by Nineteenth-Century American Men of Letters, by J. Chesley Mathews. On Reading Dante in 1965: the *Divine Comedy* as a "Bridge Across Time," by Francis Fergusson. The Relevance of the *Inferno,* by John Ciardi.

Edwin Arlington Robinson; a Reappraisal, by Louis Untermeyer. With a bibliography. 1963. 39 p. Reprinted in *Literary Lectures.*

French and German Letters Today. 1960. 53 p. Reprinted in *Literary Lectures.*

Lines of Force in French Poetry, by Pierre Emmanuel. Latest Trends in French Prose, by Alain Bosquet. Crossing the Zero Point: German Literature Since World War II, by Hans Egon Holthusen. The Modern German Mind: The Legacy of Nietzsche, by Erich Heller.

From Poe to Valéry, by T. S. Eliot. 1949. 16 p. Reprinted in *Literary Lectures*.

George Bernard Shaw, Man of the Century, by Archibald Henderson. 1957. 15 p. Reprinted in *Literary Lectures*.

Germany and the Germans, by Thomas Mann. 1946. 20 p. Reprinted in *Literary Lectures*.

Goethe and Democracy, by Thomas Mann. 1950. 28 p. Reprinted in *Literary Lectures*.

The Imagination in the Modern World. Three Lectures, by Stephen Spender. 1962. 40 p. Reprinted in *Literary Lectures*.
   The imagination as Verb. The Organic, the Orchidaceous, the Intellectualized. Imagination Means Individuation.

Literary Lectures, Presented at the Library of Congress. 1973. 602 p. LC 1.14:L71. $8.50.
   Reprints of 37 lectures on literature.

Louise Bogan: A Woman's Words, by William Jay Smith. With a bibliography. 1971. 81 p. LC 1.14:Sm6. 95 cents.

Metaphor as Pure Adventure, by James Dickey. 1968. 20 p. LC 1.14:D55/2. 40 cents.

National Poetry Festival, Held in the Library of Congress, October 22–24, 1962: Proceedings. 1964. 367 p. Out of print.

Nietzsche's Philosophy in the Light of Contemporary Events, by Thomas Mann. 1947. 37 p. Reprinted in *Literary Lectures*.

Of Human Bondage, With a Digression on the Art of Fiction, by W. Somerset Maugham. 1946. 16 p. Out of print.

Perspectives: Recent Literature of Russia, China, Italy, and Spain. 1961. 57 p. Reprinted in *Literary Lectures*.
   Russan Soviet Literature Today, by Marc Slonim. Chinese Letters Since the Literary Revolution (1917), by Lin Yutang. The Progress of Realism in the Italian Novel, by Giose Rimanelli. The Contemporary Literature of Spain, by Arturo Torres-Rioseco.

Portrait of a Poet; Hans Christian Andersen and His Fairytales, by Erik Haugaard. 1973. 17 p. LC 29.9:H29. 40 cents.

Questions to an Artist Who is Also an Author; A Conversation Between Maurice Sendak and Virginia Haviland. 1972. 18 p. LC 1.17/A:AR 78. 55 cents.
   Reprinted from the October 1971 *Quarterly Journal of the Library of Congress*, v. 28, no. 4.

Randall Jarrell, by Karl Shapiro. With a bibliography of Jarrell materials in the collections of the Library of Congress. 1967. 47 p. LC 29.9:Sh2. 70 cents.

Recent American Fiction, by Saul Bellow. 1963. 12 p. Reprinted in *Literary Lectures*.

Robert Frost: A Backward Look, by Louis Untermeyer. With a selective bibliography. 1964. 40 p. Out of print.

Saint-John Perse: Praise and Presence, by Pierre Emmanuel. With a bibliography. 1971. 82 p. LC 29.9:P43. 90 cents.

Spinning the Crystal Ball; Some Guesses at the Future of American Poetry, by James Dickey. 1967. 22 p. LC 1.14:D55. 40 cents.

The Theme of the Joseph Novels, by Thomas Mann. 1943. 23 p. Reprinted in *Literary Lectures*.

The Translation of Poetry. Address [by Allen Tate] and panel discussion presented at the International Poetry Festival held at the Library of Congress, April 13-15, 1970. 1972. 40 p. LC 29.9:T18. 60 cents.

Three Views of the Novel. 1957. 41 p. Reprinted in *Literary Lectures*.
 The Biographical Novel, by Irving Stone. Remarks on the Novel, by John O'Hara. The Historical Novel, by MacKinlay Kantor.

Two Lectures: Leftovers [by] William Stafford. From Anne to Marianne [by] Josephine Jacobsen. 1973. LC 1.14:St 1. 55 cents.

Walt Whitman: Man, Poet, Philosopher. 1955, reissued 1969. 53 p. LC 29.2:W59/2. 65 cents.
 The Man, by Gay Wilson Allen. The Poet, by Mark Van Doren. The Philosopher, by David Daiches.

The War and the Future, by Thomas Mann. 1944. 23 p. Reprinted in *Literary Lectures*.

Ways of Misunderstanding Poetry, by Reed Whittemore. 1965. 13 p. Reprinted in *Literary Lectures*.

Willa Cather: The Paradox of Success, by Leon Edel. 1960. 17 p. Reprinted in *Literary Lectures*.

The Writer's Experience. 1964. 32 p. Reprinted in *Literary Lectures*.
 Hidden Name and Complex Fate: A Writer's Experience in the United States, by Ralph Ellison. American Poet? by Karl Shapiro.

☆U.S. GOVERNMENT PRINTING OFFICE: 1975 O—552-493